the
dog owner's
manual

[front]

[left side]

[right side]

[back]

the
dog
owner's manual

OPERATING INSTRUCTIONS, TROUBLESHOOTING
TIPS, AND ADVICE ON LIFETIME MAINTENANCE

by Dr. David Brunner and Sam Stall

Illustrated by Paul Kepple and Jude Buffum

QUIRK BOOKS
PHILADELPHIA

Library of Congress Cataloging in Publication Number: 2003096236

ISBN-13: 978-1-931686-85-3

Printed in China

Typeset in Swiss

Designed by Paul Kepple and Jude Buffum @ Headcase Design
headcasedesign.com

10 9 8 7

Quirk Books
215 Church Street
Philadelphia, PA 19106
quirkbooks.com

Contents

Welcome
to Your New Dog!

[UNPACK CAREFULLY]

dog

Model: ☐ Puppy ☐ Adult
Not intended for resale

FRAGILE

THIS END UP

Contents: One (1) Jack Russell Terrier

ATTENTION!

Before beginning this manual, please inspect your model carefully. If any of the standard parts shown on pages 16–17 appear to be missing or inoperative, consult your dog's service provider immediately.

Whether you have just acquired a new dog or are contemplating getting one, congratulations. This product's legendary utility has inspired unprecedented customer loyalty among humans of every culture, age, and locale. With proper care and maintenance, it can accomplish almost any task its owner cares to assign.

The dog is surprisingly similar to other high-tech devices you may already own. Like cars, dogs are available in numerous makes and models. Like PCs, they can be configured to serve different functions. And like home security systems, they can keep you and your property safe and sound.

However, while most such highly developed consumer products come with instruction manuals, dogs do not. This is a major oversight, since the complexity of their programming far exceeds that of even the fastest computers, and their mechanical functions are more varied and subtle than those of the finest automobiles. With proper guidance, this near-autonomous system can master numerous desirable behaviors. It can even provide companionship and love. But used improperly, it can manifest traits inconvenient and/or harmful to you, your family, and your possessions.

Hence this book. *The Dog Owner's Manual* is a comprehensive user's guide that explains how to derive maximum enjoyment from your canine. It is not necessary to read it from cover to cover. For ease of use, this book has been divided into 11 sections. If you have a question or problem, turn to any of the following chapters:

OVERVIEW OF MAKES AND MODELS (pages 20–49) offers a primer on the literally hundreds of available dog types, a quick look at important hardware and software variations, and guidance on making the right choice for your lifestyle.

HOME INSTALLATION (pages 50–67) explains how to safely introduce a dog into your home and to its new human and/or animal companions.

DAILY INTERACTION (pages 68–85) covers elementary maintenance issues such as deciphering dog behavior, body language, and play preferences.

BASIC PROGRAMMING (pages 86–101) offers an overview of factory-installed software (instinctive behaviors) and owner-installed software add-ons (training).

FUEL REQUIREMENTS (pages 102–115) discusses your dog's nutritional requirements, including when to feed, what to feed, and how much to feed.

EXTERIOR MAINTENANCE (pages 116–133) explains how to handle body-work and detailing issues, including grooming, bathing, and nail clipping.

GROWTH AND DEVELOPMENT (pages 134–143) covers puppy growth milestones, neutering/spaying, and how to calculate your dog's physio-logical age.

INTERIOR MAINTENANCE (pages 144–159) explains how to monitor a dog's mechanical systems for signs of trouble and how to select an author-ized service provider for technical support. Covers everything from minor dings to major realignments.

EMERGENCY MAINTENANCE (pages 160–187) lists major medical con-ditions that may afflict canines and outlines possible treatment alternatives.

ADVANCED FUNCTIONS (pages 188–205) surveys additional program-ming options for dogs and offers a brief look at hardware modifications and reproduction.

TROUBLESHOOTING (pages 206–215) addresses frequently asked ques-tions about common software glitches, from undue aggression to exces-sive barking.

When used properly, a dog can provide its owner with endless hours of fun, companionship, and service. Remember, however, that mastering such a complex system requires energy and commitment. As you cope with training setbacks, unauthorized bodily discharges, and programming bugs, remember that the final result—a loyal, loving pet—is well worth the effort.

Congratulations and welcome to the world of dog ownership!

The Dog: Diagram and Parts List

Though canine physical attributes can vary substantially from one breed to the next, all have the same complement of preinstalled parts and capabilities. If your pet is missing one or more of the parts or systems herein described, contact an authorized service provider immediately.

The Head

Eyes: Most dog breeds come with brown or black eyes, though some varieties are fitted with blue, green, yellow, or even a combination of colors. Each eye has three eyelids—upper, lower, and a "third" lid in the inner corner. The third lid functions as a "windshield wiper," clearing dust and debris from the surface of the eye.

Ears: May come in several styles, including button, floppy, and rose ears. The "erect ear" (seen on such breeds as German shepherds and huskies) is the standard model once used by all ancient dogs.

Nose: As with the ears, the nose can take many forms and lengths. Colors can vary from black to liver; the color often lightens during winter. In general, the longer the nose the more well-developed the dog's sense of smell. Its wetness increases its effectiveness by dissolving incoming scent molecules for easy analysis. Contrary to legend, a dry nose does not necessarily indicate sickness.

Tongue: While frequently used to taste potential food, the canine tongue is also used to vent excess heat. The movement of air back and forth across its surface (via panting), combined with the evaporation of saliva, serves to regulate body temperature.

Teeth: Dogs have 42 teeth, including six pairs of incisors in front that are bracketed by two pairs of large canines. The rest are molars and premolars, allowing dogs (unlike some predators) to easily add vegetarian fare to their diets, if circumstances dictate.

The Body

Coat: All dogs, even the so-called "hairless" varieties, have a covering of fur. Its color and/or combination of colors can vary widely, even among members of the same breed. Muscles in the skin allow the hairs to stand up or "bristle." Excess shedding or a dull, brittle coat may indicate health problems. (See "Exterior Maintenance," pages 116–133.)

Output Port: The dog's waste discharge system also functions as a means for identification. The anus is bracketed by two internal anal glands that secrete a strong, pungent odor along with each bowel movement. This acts as an olfactory "calling card" to other dogs. When canines sniff each other's hindquarters, they are in fact investigating the anal glands.

Genitals: Male dogs reach sexual maturity at approximately 8 months of age. Females become sexually mature at 9 to 15 months.

Paws: Most of the dog's sense of touch is located here. Dogs can also sweat through their paw pads.

Tail: Used primarily to signal emotions. The number of bones in a dog's tail (and therefore its length) varies from animal to animal.

Nipples: These docking ports for peripherals come preinstalled on both female and male models. However, the circuitry of the male model renders these valves inoperative.

Weight: Dog weights vary markedly, from a maximum of more than 200 pounds (91 kg) to a minimum of 2 or 3 pounds (1–1.5 kg). In general, male dogs weigh about 10 percent more than females of the same breed.

Height: As with weight, canine dimensions vary wildly from breed to breed. While the Irish wolfhound stands roughly 32 inches (81 cm) tall at the shoulders, the Chihuahua can be as short as 5 inches (13 cm).

Sensor Specifications

All dogs possess a highly developed suite of environmental sensors. The data they furnish provide canines with a situational awareness far superior to that of humans.

Visual Sensors: The dog's vision is a legacy system from the wolf. It is excellent for spotting moving targets at great distances and in poor lighting.

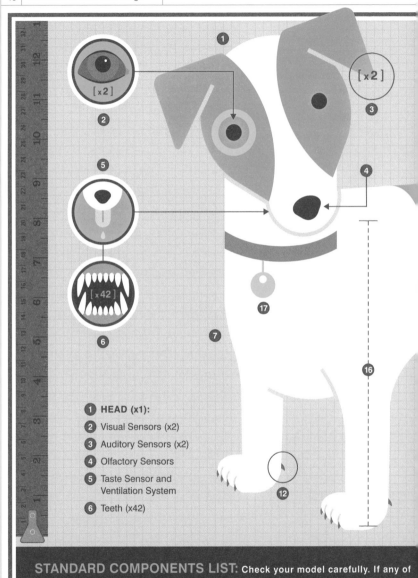

1. **HEAD (x1):**
2. Visual Sensors (x2)
3. Auditory Sensors (x2)
4. Olfactory Sensors
5. Taste Sensor and Ventilation System
6. Teeth (x42)

STANDARD COMPONENTS LIST: Check your model carefully. If any of

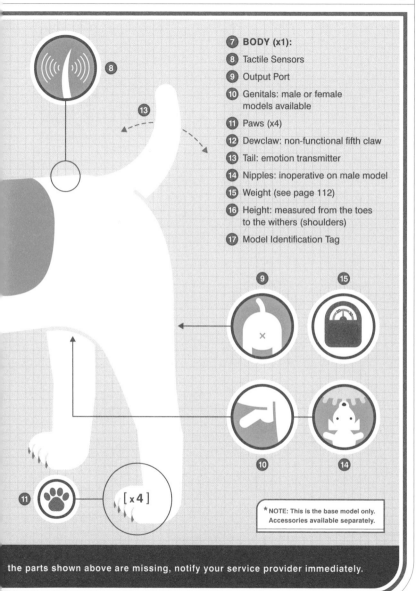

7 BODY (x1):

8 Tactile Sensors

9 Output Port

10 Genitals: male or female models available

11 Paws (x4)

12 Dewclaw: non-functional fifth claw

13 Tail: emotion transmitter

14 Nipples: inoperative on male model

15 Weight (see page 112)

16 Height: measured from the toes to the withers (shoulders)

17 Model Identification Tag

[x4]

* NOTE: This is the base model only. Accessories available separately.

the parts shown above are missing, notify your service provider immediately.

However, dogs see fewer colors than humans and cannot discern fine detail. At close range they rely heavily on their sense of smell, which is almost unequaled in the animal world.

Olfactory Sensors: While human noses contain between 5 million and 20 million scent-analyzing cells, dogs can carry 200 million or more. The bloodhound, famed for its tracking skills, possesses 300 million. To handle all this data, the olfactory processing center of a dog's brain is 40 times larger than that of humans. This faculty allows rescue dogs to detect humans buried under an avalanche and enables tracking hounds to follow scent trails that are 3 days old.

Auditory Sensors: Dog ears can move independently of each other, allowing them to pinpoint the origins of specific sounds in a fraction of a second. Dogs can also hear extremely high frequencies (as high as 40,000 cycles per second, compared to 20,000 per second for humans) and detect noises at roughly four times the range of humans. In other words, what you hear at 50 feet (15 m), a dog can hear at 200 feet (60 m).

Tactile Sensors: Each hair in a dog's coat acts as an antenna, feeding environmental data to a *mechanoreceptor* nerve at its base. This data allows the canine to be acutely aware of its immediate surroundings.

Taste Sensors: Dogs possess only about 1,700 taste buds compared to roughly 9,000 in humans. This relative lack of taste explains their undiscriminating palates, allowing them to eat almost any food without complaint (and to lick themselves without gagging).

Memory Capacity

Experts debate the exact intelligence quotient of dogs and even whether it is possible to gauge the IQ of a nonhuman species. What can be said with certainty is that the average dog's memory capacity and problem-solving skills far exceed those of the most powerful computers. Consider the fact that while supercomputers can play master-level chess, they can't begin to tackle such complex tasks as foxhunting or guiding a blind person down a city street.

Similarly, comparing the acuity of different breeds can be a very subjective exercise. Some models excel at mental traits—trainability, energy, inquisitiveness—desired by humans. This may make them appear "smarter" than other canines. However, these traits aren't always a plus. Many dogs with high "intelligence," such as Border collies and terriers, require plenty of exercise, mental stimulation, and "face time" with their owners. Conversely, allegedly less intelligent breeds can be much more laid-back and easier to live with.

Product Life Span

The operational life span of dogs averages 12 years, but your model's mileage may vary. As a rule of thumb, larger varieties depreciate much more rapidly than compact ones. For instance, a 7-year-old mastiff or Great Dane is very close to obsolescence. However, a poodle, beagle, or similar small dog could easily function twice that long or longer. The oldest documented canine life span was 29 years.

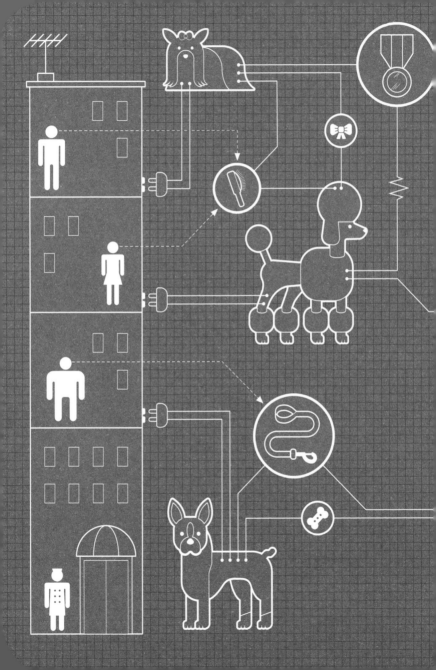

Chapter 1

Overview of
Makes and Models

A Brief Product History

Since before the dawn of civilization, dogs have been a valued and welcome component of human society. But because the animal's association with man is so ancient, we know very little about the long-gone days when it was created.

Experts theorize that the dog, or *Canis familiaris*, was developed from its wild cousin, the wolf (*Canis lupus*). Though the wolf is a far less user-friendly system (Fig. A), it carries much of the basic programming (loyalty, courage, and highly developed social skills) that humans covet in dogs. Over many generations, wolf behavior was altered by selective breeding to enhance those desirable characteristics and to suppress undesirable ones, such as extreme aggression. The result has become one of marketing's greatest success stories. Today there are approximately 60 million dogs in the United States alone (Fig. B), compared to only about 100,000 wolves worldwide.

The physical differences between *Canis familiaris* and *Canis lupus* can be quite radical. While wolves adhere to one standard physical template, dogs come in a variety of shapes and sizes. Every trait from coat length to hair color will vary from breed to breed—and from individual to individual.

The same, however, can't be said of a dog's programming. Except for a few key modifications, dogs and wolves still share the same basic operating system. For instance, a dog's willingness to cohabit with human families springs directly from its wild progenitor's preference for living and hunting in packs. The dog's legendary courage in territorial and personal defense, its ability to understand and obey instructions, even its devotion to children, are all attributes of pack behavior.

Of course, not all of the dog's undesirable programming has been deleted. Like wolves, they constantly seek to upgrade their status in the pack—usually by dominating lesser members. In the wild this means that the strongest animal leads. In a domestic situation, a dog who tries to dominate its master may become aggressive, uncontrollable, or, at the very least, annoying.

Fortunately, in most cases, these programming glitches can be fixed with careful socialization and firm discipline—both of which will be explained in upcoming pages.

CANIS LUPUS VS. CANIS FAMILIARIS

(Fig. A)
Canis lupus, 10,000 B.C.

(Fig. B)
Canis familiaris, Today

Survey of Brands

The majority of the world's dogs are undifferentiated varieties produced by random interbreeding. These are called "mixed breeds" or "mutts." However, there are also numerous selectively bred models that reliably produce a particular body type and/or emphasize specific behaviors. Dogs created in this way are called "purebreds." America's leading purebred association, the American Kennel Club, divides them into seven major groups:

Sporting Dogs: This division is composed mostly of pointers, retrievers, setters, and spaniels, including the golden retriever, Labrador retriever, Weimaraner, cocker spaniel, and Irish setter. *Best Features:* All have active, energetic personalities. *Caveat:* Members of the sporting group usually require regular, vigorous exercise.

Working Dogs: Developed for such things as guard duty and rescue work, working dogs are among the strongest and hardiest of all breeds. The list includes the Great Dane, Doberman pinscher, Alaskan malamute, Newfoundland, Saint Bernard, and Rottweiler. *Best Features:* Their courage and large size make many models in this group ideal for home defense. *Caveat:* These powerful dogs require careful training and socialization.

Toys: Members of the toy group are, for the most part, tiny. Not surprisingly, many are classic lapdogs. Toy models include the Maltese, Chihuahua, Shih Tzu, Pekingese, and Pomeranian. *Best Features:* Perfect for apartment dwellers with little space to spare. ***Caveat:*** Not all lapdogs are placid. Chihuahuas and Pomeranians, in particular, can present numerous behavioral challenges.

Terriers: Developed to pursue, corner, and kill everything from rats to badgers, members of the terrier group are famous for their distinctive (some would say *challenging*) personalities. These energetic dogs are best-suited to an energetic owner. Models include the cairn terrier, Jack Russell terrier, bull terrier, Border terrier, and the American Staffordshire terrier. ***Best Features:*** Terriers are known for their vitality and colorful attitudes. ***Caveat:*** They can be very combative with other dogs and may try to dominate an overly passive owner.

Hounds: A loose grouping encompassing several models originally designed for hunting animals in open country, most are now utilized primarily as house pets. The hound group includes the beagle, basset hound, Rhodesian ridgeback, greyhound, and borzoi. ***Best Features:*** When not actually hunting, many hound models display placid, laid-back personalities. ***Caveat:*** Some hounds, such as beagles, regularly emit a loud, drawn-out bark/howl called a "bay." Learn if the particular model you desire does this, and experience it for yourself, before acquiring one.

Nonsporting Dogs: A catchall category that includes breeds of diverse size, shape, and temperament, these dogs are best defined by what they *aren't* (not a hound, not a terrier, not a working dog) rather than what they are. Well-

known nonsporting models include the bichon frise, bulldog, poodle, and Dalmatian. ***Best Features:*** From guard dogs to lapdogs, this group offers models for every lifestyle. ***Caveat:*** The diversity of this category makes generalizations about behavior and/or physical requirements impossible.

Herding Dogs: As the name implies, all members of this group excel at controlling the movements of other animals. The group includes the collie, Border collie, Old English sheepdog, and the Welsh corgi (a tiny, slow-moving model that nevertheless can herd cattle by nipping at their heels). ***Best Features:*** Many herding breeds, such as the Border collie, are renowned for their intelligence and energy. ***Caveat:*** When it comes to herding dogs, the line between "intelligent and energetic" and "nervous and high-strung" can be very thin. If a herder does not receive regular, stimulating exercise, it may "exercise itself" by destroying your personal property.

Top-Selling Models

Though there are hundreds of dog breeds, a relative handful enjoy near-universal popularity and acceptance. The following models are either extremely common or so well-known that they merit special mention. If any interest you, consult a veterinarian or local breed club for more information. Always buy a purebred from a reputable breeder.

Akita Inu: Originally bred for fighting and guarding, the Akita is the national dog of Japan. ***Height:*** 25–28 inches (64–71 cm). ***Weight:*** 66–100 pounds (34–45 kg). ***Exterior:*** Thick coated; strong resemblance to Western working breeds such as German shepherds and huskies; powerfully built with a curling, bristly tail. **Best Features:** High intelligence and loyalty to master. **Caveat:** Can dominate a weak owner. Aggressive toward other dogs. **Special Programming:** Excellent memory. **Ideal Owner:** Strong, energetic person willing to satisfy the Akita's need for exercise and firm handling.

American Staffordshire Terrier: Originally bred for pit fighting and bull baiting, it is, pound for pound, arguably the strongest dog in the world. **Height:** 16–18 inches (41–46 cm). **Weight:** 37–44 pounds (17–20 kg). **Exterior:** Short, smooth coat in a variety of colors. Extremely powerfully built, with a barrel chest, obvious muscle development, and extra-wide jaws. **Best Features:** Properly bred models make steady, loyal companions. **Caveat:** A poorly bred model in the hands of an abusive or otherwise incompetent owner can be extremely dangerous. **Special Programming:** Indifferent to pain, completely fearless. **Ideal Owner:** Strong, energetic person capable of developing this model's tender side.

Basset Hound: A descendant of the bloodhound, the basset's short legs were developed so human hunters could stand a better chance of keeping up with it in the field. **Height:** 15 inches (38 cm). **Weight:** 40–51 pounds (18–23 kg). **Exterior:** Short, smooth coat, short legs, long ears that can drag on the ground. **Best Features:** Patient to a fault, devoted to its family, good with children, all but incapable of aggression. **Caveat:** Can be difficult to house-train—or to train at all. **Special Programming:** The basset's sense of smell is one of the dog world's keenest. **Ideal Owner:** A person who will give it proper exercise (bassets gain weight easily) and plenty of personal attention.

Beagle: One of the oldest European hunting models, it dates at least to the 14th century. **Height:** 13–16 inches (33–41 cm). **Weight:** 26–33 pounds

(12–15 kg). **Exterior:** Smooth coat, floppy ears. **Best Features:** Good with children and families; shows almost no aggression. **Caveat:** Easily distracted. If it catches an interesting scent, an unleashed beagle will simply vanish. Also, they tend to overeat. **Special Programming:** Beagles announce the arrival of strangers with a hair-raising, drawn-out bark/howl called a "bay." **Ideal Owner:** A family with children.

Boxer: So-named because of its alleged proclivity for rearing onto its hind legs and "boxing" with its forearms. **Height:** 21–25 inches (53–63 cm). **Weight:** 53–70 pounds (24–32 kg). **Exterior:** Short, smooth coat, well-muscled body, flat nose, and an intimidating facial expression. **Best Features:** An excellent watchdog, but also good with children. **Caveat:** Has a relatively short life span (usually less than 10 years). **Special Programming:** The boxer, though exuberant, tends to display much less aggression than other popular guarding breeds, such as the German shepherd and Rottweiler. **Ideal Owner:** A family with children.

Chihuahua: Arguably developed in pre-Colombian Mexico, it is the world's smallest dog breed. **Height:** 5–9 inches (15–23 cm). **Weight:** 1–6 pounds (.5–3 kg). **Exterior:** Coat can be short or long. Head shapes include "deer" (longish face with well-developed muzzle) and "apple" (large eyes, large skull, shortened muzzle) varieties. **Best Features:** This sprightly dog has a fiery, entertaining personality. It is also an excellent watchdog. **Caveat:** Its small stature makes it somewhat fragile. Mature dogs have a small opening in the tops of their skulls, making them vulnerable to head injury. **Special Programming:** Chihuahuas don't seem to realize how little they are. They will, without hesitation, attack dogs 20 times their size. *Do not allow them to do this.* **Ideal Owner:** Apartment dwellers and senior citizens.

Collie: Originally developed in the Scottish Highlands as a herding dog. *Height:* 22–24 inches (56–61 cm). *Weight:* 48–70 pounds (22–32 kg). *Exterior:* One of the most aesthetically pleasing of all dogs, collies' luxurious coats come in sable, tricolor, and blue merle patterns. A shorthaired "smooth" model is also available. *Best Features:* A steady, highly intelligent dog. *Caveat:* Can be somewhat tricky to train—headstrong, yet also sensitive and timid. *Special Programming:* Collies, originally developed to herd, often seize any opportunity to implement this portion of their programming. They have been known to "herd" children, other pets, even groups of adults. *Ideal Owner:* Anyone willing to shoulder the prodigious costs of grooming (and who doesn't mind having large amounts of sable, tricolor, or blue merle hairs on their home furnishings).

Dachshund: Developed to hunt prey in its lair, the dachshund's name means "badger dog." *Height:* 8–10 inches (20–25 cm). *Weight:* 12–15 pounds (5–7 kg). *Exterior:* This short-legged, long-bodied model comes in longhaired, shorthaired, and wirehaired varieties. *Best Features:* A well-tempered dog with few programming glitches. *Caveat:* Can be problematic around children. Resistant to training. *Special Programming:* Dachshunds were designed to be fearless hunters. Though they resemble lapdogs, they act like terriers. Owners expecting a placid couch companion will be disappointed. *Ideal Owner:* A person willing to invest the time to train a dachshund properly.

Doberman Pinscher: Developed in the 1860s by a German dogcatcher named Louis Dobermann. *Height:* 27–28 inches (69–71 cm). *Weight:* 66–88 pounds (30–40 kg). *Exterior:* Short, smooth, mostly black coat (though color variations such as blue and red are available). Powerfully muscled, graceful body. Floppy ears that are sometimes "cropped" to a point. *Best Features:* A peerless, highly disciplined guard dog. *Caveat:*

models shown above (and on pages 36–37) represent some of the most popular canines.

Can be very aggressive if not handled properly. **Special Programming:** Dobermans are extremely intelligent and can accept a great deal of complicated training. Males can be markedly more aggressive than females. **Ideal Owner:** An experienced handler who can offer thorough training and consistent discipline. These dogs are not intended for novices.

German Shepherd: Originally developed as a herding dog. **Height:** 22–26 inches (56–66 cm). **Weight:** 62–77 pounds (28–35 kg). **Exterior:** Most commonly a short, tan coat with a black "saddle" across the back. However, solid black models are available (along with other color combinations), plus medium-haired and longhaired varieties. **Best Features:** Highly intelligent and trainable. **Caveat:** Coat sheds perpetually. **Special Programming:** Shepherds love to work and excel at everything from guarding to rescue. **Ideal Owner:** Someone who can give the dog plenty to do—and can control its natural aggressive tendencies.

Golden Retriever: The entire breed reportedly stems from the 19th-century pairing of a yellow wavy-coated retriever to a Tweed water spaniel. **Height:** 20–24 inches (51–61 cm). **Weight:** 59–81 pounds (27–37 kg). **Exterior:** Straight or slightly wavy golden coat. Friendly, perpetually pleasant expression. **Best Features:** Amiable, playful, and gentle, the golden is a family dog without peer. **Caveat:** It is completely useless for personal protection or home defense. **Special Programming:** Originally bred as a hunting dog, it is still sometimes used for that purpose. **Ideal Owner:** Anyone willing to give it the attention and daily exercise it requires.

Greyhound: The fastest of all dogs, it can run at speeds exceeding 40 mph (64 kmph). **Height:** 27–31 inches (69–79 cm). **Weight:** 55–66 pounds (25–30 kg). **Exterior:** Short coat in a variety of shades. Lithe, powerfully built body.

Best Features: Though famous for its explosive speed, the greyhound also makes a docile, well-mannered pet. *Caveat:* Greyhounds need a great deal of exercise. *Special Programming:* The urge to pursue game is so deeply ingrained that no amount of remedial work can overcome it. Greyhounds must always be leashed in public. They are easily distracted by moving objects and/or small animals (including cats), which they may chase over great distances and—if not stopped—kill. *Ideal Owner:* An athletic person willing to give the dog the exercise it needs.

Jack Russell Terrier: Developed in the 19th century by English clergyman and dog breeder Parson Jack Russell. *Height:* 13–14 inches (33–36 cm). *Weight:* 9–18 pounds (4–8 kg). *Exterior:* Available in wirehaired and smooth-coated versions. Body shape, leg length, and facial structure vary far more widely from individual to individual than is generally seen in a recognized breed. *Best Features:* A highly intelligent, breathtakingly athletic companion dog with one of the canine world's most vivacious personalities. *Caveat:* Possibly the most belligerent and high-tempered of all terriers. *Special Programming:* Jacks were originally bred to chase game into (or out of) underground lairs. As such, they are adept at pursuit, fighting, and digging up back yards. *Ideal Owner:* An experienced dog owner who can supply the extensive training and firm hand this model requires.

Labrador Retriever: The most popular dog model in the United States. *Height:* 21–24 inches (53–61 cm). *Weight:* 55–79 pounds (25–36 kg). *Exterior:* Available in black, chocolate, and yellow. To facilitate swimming, its coat is waterproof and its toes are webbed. *Best Features:* Excellent family dog. Loves children. Accepting of guests. *Caveat:* No guarding skills whatsoever. Tends to overeat. *Special Programming:* Because Labradors were designed to retrieve game from the water, they love to swim and get wet. ***Ideal Owner:*** A family with lakefront property and a very high tolerance for the game of fetch.

Newfoundland: A working dog once used by fishermen to carry burdens and to help haul in nets. ***Height:*** 26–28 inches (66–71 cm). ***Weight:*** 99–150 pounds (45–68 kg). ***Exterior:*** Long, waterproof black or brown coat. Massive, stocky body and webbed toes to facilitate swimming. ***Best Features:*** Though its size and phenomenal strength make it intimidating, the Newfoundland is, in fact, quite mellow, making it a good family dog. ***Caveat:*** "Newfies" drool excessively and their coats require regular, careful grooming. ***Special Programming:*** Because of their strength and affinity for the water, Newfoundlands are sometimes employed as water rescue dogs. ***Ideal Owner:*** A family with a large house and yard. Newfoundlands are not apartment dwellers.

Pekingese: Formerly a fixture at the imperial Chinese court, it was brought to the West in the 19th century. ***Height:*** 6–9 inches (15–23 cm). ***Weight:*** 10–13 pounds (5–6 kg). ***Exterior:*** Long, silky coat with a black face surrounded by a lionlike mane. Available in numerous colors. ***Best Features:*** The dog displays a placid demeanor and devotes itself to its master. ***Caveat:*** Has little patience with children. Obedience training is very difficult, if not impossible. ***Special Programming:*** Although "Pekes" are difficult to train, their basic temperament is easygoing and cooperative. They generally avoid trouble. ***Ideal Owner:*** Anyone who wants a small dog to dote on.

Poodle: Originally a hunting dog with a strong affinity for water, its name derives from the German word *pudeln*, which means "splash." These dogs come in four different sizes: standard, medium, miniature, and toy. ***Height:*** Standard, 18–23 inches (46–58 cm); Medium, 14–18 inches (36–46 kg); Miniature, 11–14 inches (28–36 cm); Toy, up to 10 inches (25 cm). ***Weight:***

Standard, 48 pounds (22 kg); Medium, 26 pounds (12 kg); Miniature, 15 pounds (7 kg); Toy, up to 11 pounds (5 kg). *Exterior:* All possess thick, woolly coats that come in a variety of shades. *Best Features:* Poodles are highly intelligent with amiable, steady personalities. *Caveat:* Though most poodles are famously even-tempered, toys and miniatures display a tendency to bite. *Special Programming:* Besides being intelligent, poodles are eager to learn and easy to train. *Ideal Owner:* Virtually anyone.

Pug: Legend says that the pug was brought to Europe by Genghis Khan. *Height:* 10–12 inches (25–30 cm). *Weight:* 14–18 pounds (6–8 kg). *Exterior:* Short, smooth coat in silver, black, or beige, but always with a black face. Pushed-in nose and large, expressive eyes. Very stocky body. *Best Features:* An entertaining little dog that makes few physical or psychological demands on its owner. Good with children. *Caveat:* Given to loud, relentless snoring. *Special Programming:* Adaptable to almost any living arrangement, from a small apartment with one resident to a large house full of children. *Ideal Owner:* Anyone who can tolerate snoring.

Shih Tzu: A Chinese dog, possibly a cross between a Pekingese and a Lhasa apso. *Height:* 8–11 inches (20–28 cm). *Weight:* 9–16 pounds (4–7 kg). *Exterior:* Long, silky hair in a variety of shades. *Best Features:* The perfect lapdog—just as it was in China, where it was a favorite of the imperial court. *Caveat:* Other than for cuddling, it has no particular talents. *Special Programming:* Very placid personality; devoted to its owner. *Ideal Owner:* Anyone seeking a low-maintenance dog. Everything about the Shih Tzu (except its coat) is low maintenance.

Yorkshire Terrier: Originally developed in Yorkshire, England, to rid coal mines of rats. *Height:* 7–9 inches (18–23 cm). *Weight:* 7 pounds (3 kg). *Exterior:*

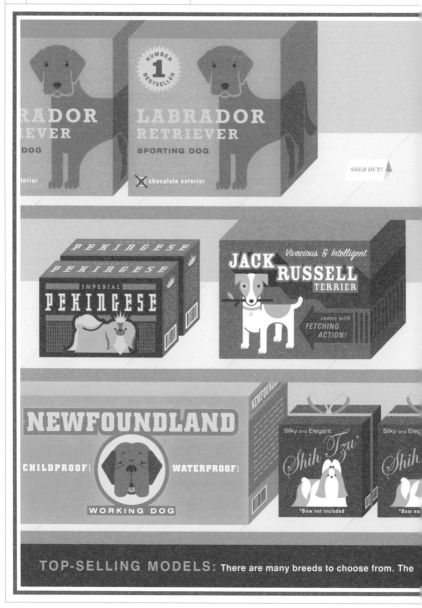

TOP-SELLING MODELS: There are many breeds to choose from. The

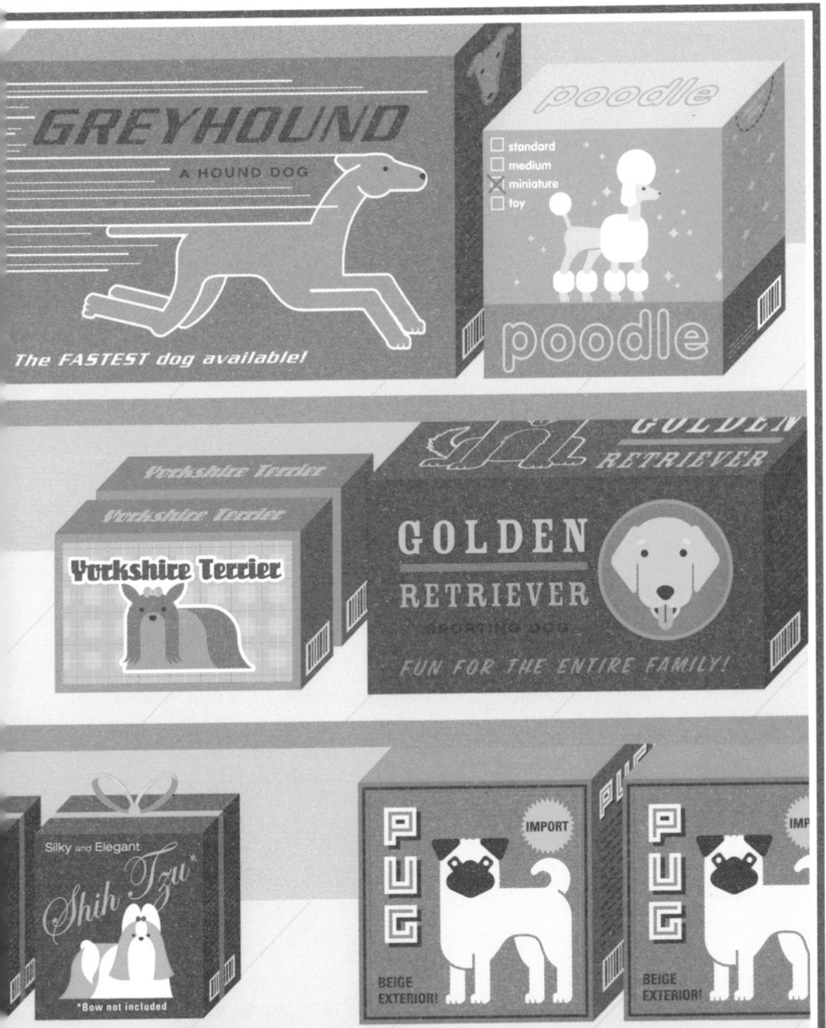

models shown above (and on pages 30–31) represent some of the most popular canines.

Long, shiny, finely textured coat that is golden on the head, chest, and legs, but is steel blue everywhere else. ***Best Features:*** A happy, lively dog with all the spirit of bigger terriers. ***Caveat:*** Will try to attack much larger dogs. Can be difficult to train. Hair (if kept long) requires regular grooming. ***Special Programming:*** "Yorkies" only look like lapdogs. Inside they carry the same aggressive, energetic programming as other terriers. ***Ideal Owner:*** Anyone willing to undertake the management of a very energetic dog.

Nonstandard, Off-Brand Models

There are more than 500 dog breeds, but their numbers are dwarfed by the worldwide population of mixed breeds, or mutts. Available primarily through informal distribution channels (private owners, animal shelters), their highly individualized software packages and mechanical layouts carry both advantages and disadvantages. While the programming of a purebred is designed to accentuate one or more behaviors (herding in a Border collie, territoriality in a German shepherd), a mutt's programming is not. Temperaments and skill sets vary; the only way to discover what a particular model offers is to study it closely.

Conversely, mutts enjoy some important mechanical advantages. The controlled breeding that accentuates certain physical and mental traits in purebreds also magnifies genetic defects, predisposing them to everything from hip problems to various skin conditions. Mutts, because of their cosmopolitan genetic makeup, display few such weaknesses.

If you're interested in a specific, very expensive breed, one option is to select a mutt that obviously incorporates traits from that model (based on a visual inspection or data supplied by its current owner) into its lineage. With luck, you can get all the positive characteristics of the desired model in a healthier, more affordable animal.

EXAMPLES OF MIXED BREEDS

(Fig. A)
"DARBY"

Doberman
42%

Pekingese
11%

Pug
47%

(Fig. B)
"HUXLEY"

Akita
23%

Boston Terrier
31%

Schnauzer
46%

(Fig. C)
"POMPOM"

Basset Hound
9%

Dachshund
49%

Poodle
42%

(Fig. D)
"GIZMO"

Collie
26%

Shih Tzu
58%

Yorkie
16%

Selecting an Appropriate Model

Picking the right model from such an extensive product line takes careful deliberation. To determine what breed, size, and temperament is right for you, consider the following factors:

Size: As a rule of thumb, bigger breeds are inappropriate if you live in a small apartment or a home with a small or unfenced yard. However, this is not always the case. Some more-relaxed large models, such as the golden retriever, are better suited for small spaces than, say, an energetic schnauzer. When selecting a breed, temperament and activity level are equally as important as size.

Coat Type: Longhaired breeds usually shed prodigiously and require regular, costly, professional grooming. Shorthaired varieties require less maintenance, though they can shed just as much. Dog dander (tiny skin flakes) can also aggravate human allergies. Some models, such as poodles, are less troublesome in this regard.

Temperament: Since purebreds display well-understood mental characteristics, it is important to pick a model that complements your lifestyle. Consult breed guides and also, if possible, spend time with someone who already owns the type you're considering. It is especially important to spend preacquisition time with a mutt, so you can gauge its mental properties. If its parents appear to be two related breeds, then determining its personality may be straightforward. A model of more diverse parentage (say, a German shepherd and a terrier) may be tougher to evaluate.

Physical Requirements: If you like outdoor activities and want your dog to tag along, consider a large, sporting breed or energetic terrier. If you enjoy watching sports on TV rather than playing them, consider a model that makes fewer physical demands.

Schedule Demands: During workdays, will you return home at regular hours to provide your dog with exercise and bathroom breaks? Remember that while some models (Shetland sheepdog, bloodhound, and golden retriever) don't mind being left alone, many (including Border collies and wheaten terriers) can suffer separation anxiety. (See "Behavioral/Psychological Disorders," page 178.)

Familial Considerations: Before acquiring a dog, make sure every member of the family wants to own one. Remember that models predisposed to biting or aggressive behavior are, in most cases, inappropriate for families with younger children. Also, consider the reactions of pets you already own.

Financial Obligations: Dog ownership is an ongoing expense. Food, veterinary bills, grooming, and other costs will require hundreds of dollars annually. If that price seems too steep, consider more affordable pets such as parakeets or gerbils.

⚠️ CAUTION: *Adding a dog to one's home is a life-changing decision requiring careful forethought. For that reason, canines must never, ever be given as unexpected gifts to third parties. Animal shelters euthanize such "surprises" by the hundreds of thousands each year.*

Advantages of Dog Ownership

The psychological benefits of owning a canine are well known. A carefully trained animal companion can offer fellowship, unconditional love, and often a friendship as intimate as any human bond. Dogs can also become an integral part of the family. Indeed, most adults, when asked to recall their earliest memories, will usually mention an encounter with their dog.

Canines also assist us during crises by helping to bear our emotional and psychological baggage. This function has important physiological benefits as well. Studies show that owning a dog—or even being near one—lowers human blood pressure and decreases stress levels. Over the long term this can prevent heart disease and lower health care costs, because dog owners make fewer doctor visits. A good-natured dog can also help fight depression and loneliness—one of the reasons they are used extensively to visit nursing homes and hospitals. Considering the benefits, the relatively nominal cost of keeping a dog seems like a wise investment.

New Versus Used Models

Puppies

Advantages: A puppy's programming can (to a certain degree) be modified to suit your needs. Puppies also have an easier time adjusting to new surroundings and accepting family members. *Disadvantages:* Training a puppy can be a difficult, time-consuming, and expensive task. Destruction can be considerable, ranging from carpet stains during house-training to chew-damaged furniture and mangled personal belongings.

Adult Dogs

Advantages: Quality adult dogs are usually "plug-and-play systems" equipped with all the software (housebreaking, socialization, rudimentary obedience training) necessary for family life. *Disadvantages:* Adult dogs may have trouble adjusting to new surroundings. Also, some models may carry deeply encoded software "glitches" (excessive aggression, destructive behavior) either hardwired or mistakenly installed by a previous owner.

The dog should be carefully screened for such problems before acquisition. An obedience expert or veterinarian can assess how much work would be necessary to bring the canine up to spec.

Selecting a Gender

In general (though there can be exceptions), female dogs tend to be less territorial and aggressive than males. However, having a male dog neutered (which should be done under almost all circumstances) in many cases mitigates these behaviors. Female dogs are also somewhat easier to train. This does not, however, mean that all females of all breeds are passive and pliant. For instance, though a female Rottweiler may be less aggressive and assertive than her male counterpart, she will still be far more aggressive and assertive than most other dogs of any breed.

Selecting a Vendor

Numerous individuals and agencies offer dogs for sale or adoption. Often, depending on your needs, it is possible to acquire a well-trained model at little or no initial expense.

Animal Shelters

Advantages: Shelters offer a wide choice of pre-owned models, many already user-friendly and configured for immediate home use. These facilities usually screen their stock (which ranges from mutts to the most exclusive purebreds) for undesirable traits; they will also conduct a careful physical inspection. Fees for these animals (especially when compared to those charged by pet stores and breeders) are generally nominal. Some facilities may require a waiting period, background check, and/or proof that you will have the animal spayed or neutered, if necessary. ***Disadvantages:*** None. The only important thing to remember is that the personality of a shelter dog should be carefully evaluated. Be aware that most are surrendered not for any fault of their own, but because of their owners' ignorance of canine care as well as changing lifestyles and/or pet preferences.

Pet Stores

Advantages: These businesses can be found in almost every large shopping mall. ***Disadvantages:*** Purebreds sold by pet stores can be of questionable lineage and in poor health. In spite of this, they are usually sold for premium prices. Since they are raised in a confined space, they are often poorly socialized and extremely difficult to house-train. For this reason, most dog experts advise against patronizing these establishments. At the very least, puppies purchased in such places should be carefully inspected by a veterinarian for physical and mental defects.

Breeders

Advantages: A qualified breeder (consult a veterinarian or a local or national breed club to find one in your area) is often the best source for carefully raised purebred puppies. They can often answer even the most detailed questions about your model's ancestry, genetic foibles, and personality. ***Disadvantages:*** Make sure you find a *qualified* breeder. Such a person will allow you to inspect his facility; supply the names of previous customers; offer detailed information about your puppy and its lineage; ensure that the puppy has received all vaccinations and medical care appropriate for its age; and include a written guarantee of its good health. If any of these items are lacking, find someone else.

Breed Rescue Groups

Advantages: These organizations devote themselves to "rescuing" owner-less dogs of specific breeds and then finding them new homes. The Internet provides information on numerous such groups specializing in everything from Jack Russell terriers to Newfoundlands. They are an excellent resource for those in search of a specific model. *Disadvantages:* The particular animal you want may not be in your area, so adopting it might necessitate travel.

Private Individuals

Advantages: Newspapers are full of advertisements for puppies. These are usually mixed breeds, offered "free to a good home" or for a nominal fee. In many cases such pets make fine animal companions—provided you carefully examine the puppies, their surroundings, and, if possible, their parents. (See "Puppy Preacquisition Inspection Checklist," page 46.) *Disadvantages:* In some cases, such litters may not have received veterinary care or proper socialization. Also, they increase the already-serious problem of pet overpopulation. If you do nothing else, encourage the owner to have the mother (and father, if possible) spayed and/or neutered.

EXPERT TIP: If your own dog has not been spayed or neutered, have this done immediately or as soon as feasible. (See "Sexual Maturity," page 141.)

Puppy Preacquisition Inspection

When examining a puppy, ask yourself the following questions. Ideally, all of your

◯ Yes
◯ No

If possible, inspect the puppy's mother. Is she free of major physical and/or mental shortcomings that might be passed to her offspring? (Remember that a puppy will look and behave like its parents.)

◯ Yes
◯ No

Is the puppy at least 8 weeks old? (Puppies younger than 8 weeks should not be separated from their mother and siblings.)

◯ Yes
◯ No

Does the puppy seem alert, happy, and eager to socialize with you? (A shy, withdrawn puppy may grow up to be a shy, withdrawn dog.)

◯ Yes
◯ No

Does the puppy seem gentle and amiable? (Be extremely wary of a dog that shows undue aggressive tendencies—growling, determined biting—at such an early age. This can indicate a significant software glitch.)

◯ Yes
◯ No

Has the puppy received all vaccinations and/or medical care appropriate for its age? (See "Visiting Your Service Provider," page 149.)

◯ Yes
◯ No

Is the puppy's stool firm? (A stool exam for intestinal parasites should be done by 8 weeks of age. A thin puppy may be malnourished or have worms.)

◯ Yes
◯ No

Are its eyes clear and free of discharge?

Checklist

answers should be "yes." Even a single "no" should be cause for careful consideration.

◯ Yes ◯ No	**Are its ears and nose free of discharge?**
◯ Yes ◯ No	**Is its coat clean and shiny?**
◯ Yes ◯ No	**Is its breathing regular, with no coughing and/or wheezing?**
◯ Yes ◯ No	**Is its body physically sound, with no lameness or tenderness anywhere?**

It is also important to make sure the puppy is screened for the specific genetic disorders (hip dysplasia, heart disease, blindness, etc.) common to its breed. Finally, no matter what sort of dog you plan to acquire, you should make any sale contingent on an examination and approval by your veterinarian. Detecting a heart murmur, orthopedic problem, or some other major malfunction at this early stage allows you to return the puppy before becoming emotionally attached.

⚠ **CAUTION:** *If you have young children, wait until they are at least 6 years old before acquiring a very large dog. Also, remember that the workload associated with caring for a new puppy can be similar to that required for supporting a human infant. The premature addition of a puppy to a family with very young children may trigger overload and breakdown of the home's primary caregiver.*

Adult Dog Preacquisition Inspection

When examining an adult dog, ask yourself the following questions. Ideally, all of your

○ Yes
○ No
Can you contact the dog's previous owner?

○ Yes
○ No
Is there any record of the dog's previous history and why it is being offered for sale/adoption?

○ Yes
○ No
Are you sure the dog isn't being given up by its previous owner because of aggression and/or destructiveness? (This is not necessarily a deal breaker. In many cases, loving attention and proper obedience training can clear up bad habits.)

○ Yes
○ No
Is the dog housebroken?

○ Yes
○ No
Does the dog seem friendly, amiable, and interested in you?

○ Yes
○ No
If the dog will live among children, was it raised with any?

○ Yes
○ No
Has the dog received appropriate medical care? Are there records to prove it?

○ Yes
○ No
Is the dog's stool firm?

Checklist

answers should be "yes." Even a single "no" should be cause for careful consideration.

◯ Yes ◯ No	**Are its eyes clear and free of discharge?**
◯ Yes ◯ No	**Are its ears and nose free of discharge?**
◯ Yes ◯ No	**Is its coat clean and shiny?**
◯ Yes ◯ No	**Is its breathing regular, with no coughing and/or wheezing?**
◯ Yes ◯ No	**Is its body physically sound, with no lameness or tenderness anywhere?**

Plan to spend considerable time with an adult dog before adoption, to make sure you understand its personality. Additionally, take the dog to a veterinarian for a pre-adoption checkup. Finally, remember that many of the canines surrendered to animal shelters are there not for insoluble problems, but due to their owners' ignorance and/or unwillingness to provide adequate training. A firm, loving hand could upgrade them to superior pets.

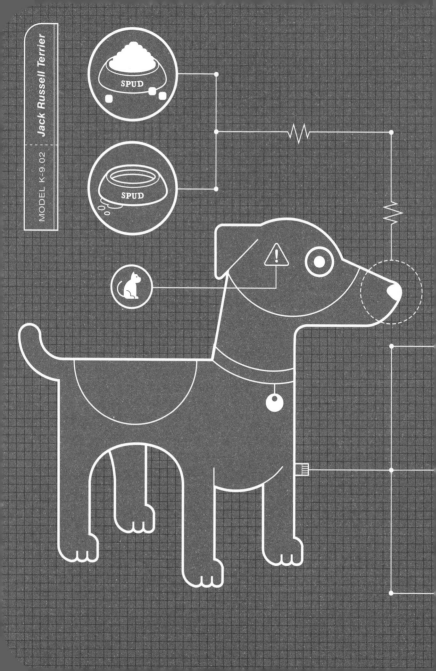

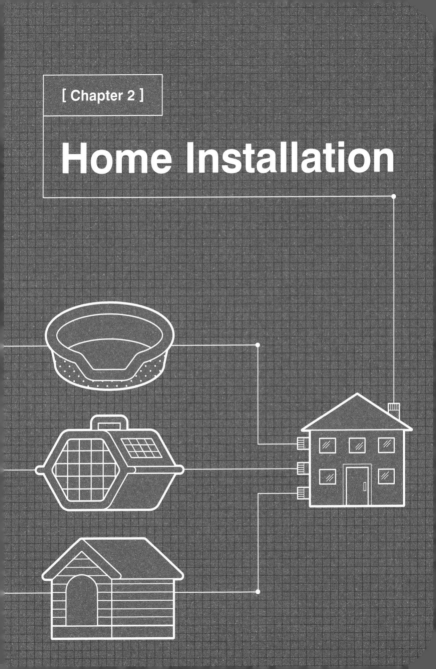

[Chapter 2]

Home Installation

Bringing a new dog into your home can be an exhilarating, albeit disruptive, experience. If your model is a puppy, you may face weeks of complex software downloads (otherwise known as "training"), plus maintenance of its complicated and ever-changing physical plant. While in most cases adult dogs don't require this level of commitment, they still need firm guidance as they find their place in a new setting. For this reason it is advisable, if possible, to stay home with your new canine during its first two or three days.

Preparing the Home

Before bringing the dog into your home, it is recommended that you take the following precautions:

■ Make sure all household cleaning products are put away.

■ Secure all medications (drugs such as Motrin and Tylenol can cause fatal liver damage in dogs).

■ Secure all unauthorized foods (chocolate, for instance, can be deadly to canines).

■ Secure all toxic chemicals stowed in your laundry room, basement, and garage—particularly antifreeze, which dogs find attractive because of its sweetness. Even a small amount, if ingested, can be lethal.

- Secure tight spaces (such as the area behind your refrigerator) where a puppy or small dog might get stuck.
- Position electrical cords out of reach so puppies cannot chew them.
- If you own a swimming pool, make sure the dog cannot fall in.
- Secure (at least for a while) any clothing, heirloom furniture, or family artifacts that should not be chewed and/or urinated upon.
- Secure houseplants, some of which (such as philodendron) are toxic.

Recommended Accessories

Commercial retailers offer thousands of products designed to complement the life cycle of standard puppies and adult dogs. While a great number of these add-ons are not mandatory, most owners choose to invest in the following:

Bed: A purpose-made cushion (perhaps stuffed with flea-repelling cedar shavings) is a good choice. Be sure the outer covering can be removed for laundering. Avoid wicker baskets; some dogs like to chew on them. Also avoid investing in an expensive dog bed until you learn whether your dog likes to destroy bedding. In the interim, old blankets and/or a pillow will suffice.

Toys: Fleece toys are excellent for puppies. Adult canines appreciate hard rubber balls (choose one that is too large to swallow or become lodged in the dog's mouth). Avoid real bones (which may splinter) or household items such as old shoes, which may convey the idea that *all* shoes are for chewing.

Comb and/or Brush: Different types are available for various coat styles. (See "General Coat Maintenance," page 122.)

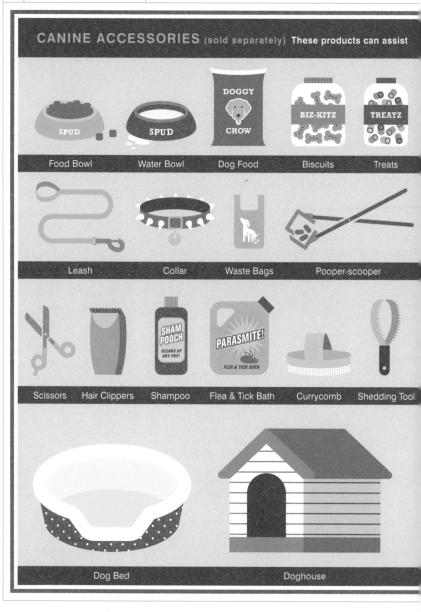

CANINE ACCESSORIES (sold separately) **These products can assist**

with the installation, handling, and maintenance of your canine.

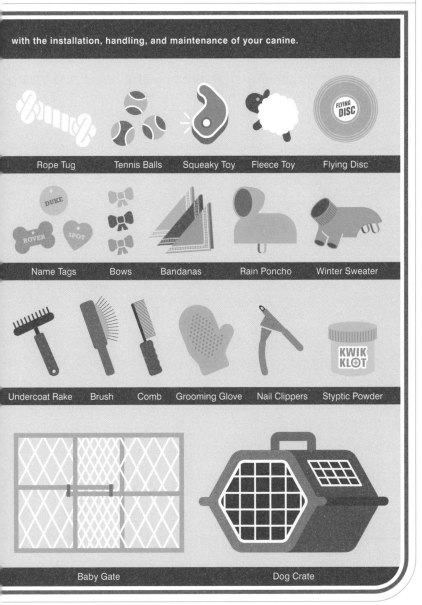

Rope Tug	Tennis Balls	Squeaky Toy	Fleece Toy	Flying Disc
Name Tags	Bows	Bandanas	Rain Poncho	Winter Sweater
Undercoat Rake	Brush	Comb	Grooming Glove	Nail Clippers	Styptic Powder

Baby Gate

Dog Crate

Collar/Tag: Put a leather or nylon collar on your dog, along with a tag containing its name and (at least) your telephone number, as soon as you acquire the animal. (See "Dog Identification Methods," page 73.)

Leash: This essential item is available at any pet store. Nylon models, which are lighter and less expensive than leather leashes, are a good choice.

Water/Food Bowls: Rubber-rimmed, stainless steel, nonskid models are best. For larger breeds or dogs with long ears, consider bowls that are elevated off the ground. Puppies may need a set of smaller, "starter" bowls.

Dog Crate: Select a model with a metal grate and a high-impact plastic body. It should be large enough for the dog, when fully grown, to turn around in. (See "Crate Training," page 81.)

Initial Introduction

Upon arriving home, offer the dog (who will undoubtedly be nervous) an immediate bathroom break. Then show it the location of its water and food bowls and encourage it to drink. However, do not offer food at this time.

Next, allow the dog several hours to explore the house under your supervision. Interface with children, other pets, and strangers should be avoided or minimized during this process. In adult dogs, expect some stress-triggered behavior regression—waste elimination "accidents," hiding, excessive shyness. Do not scold or correct a dog who acts in this way. The behaviors should vanish in a few days as the animal gains confidence in its new surroundings.

⚠ **EXPERT TIP:** *A newly adopted adult dog may act extremely reserved for several days or even weeks while adjusting to its new environment. As it becomes more comfortable, its natural personality will reassert itself.*

Interfacing with Children

Once the dog has gained a certain amount of familiarity with its new surroundings, you may begin the process of introducing it to younger human members of your family. This process should be handled in one of two ways, depending on whether the dog is a puppy or an adult. Refer to the illustrations on pages 58–59 for additional guidance.

Puppies

■ Puppies tend to squirm and can easily be dropped by children (Fig. A). Have the child sit, then hand him or her the canine (Fig. B).

■ Have the child present the puppy with a toy while holding it (Fig. C). Puppies tend to chew, and a toy may prevent them from nibbling on tiny fingers and arms.

■ Encourage the child to feed and water the puppy (Fig. C). This will increase bonding. However, remember that adults are always ultimately responsible for the canine's health and maintenance.

■ Stay in the room. Very young children (1–6 years old) should always be closely supervised when handling a puppy.

■ If the children are approximately 10 years or older, they should participate in the puppy's obedience training.

Adult Dogs

■ Leash the dog during initial introduction. At first glance, a larger dog may perceive small children as potential prey (Fig. D).

CHILD ---> ADULT DOG INTERFACE

(Fig. D)
LEASH DOG DURING INTRODUCTION

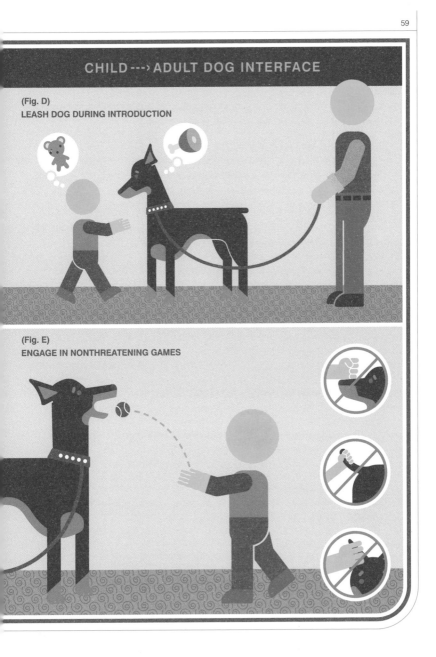

(Fig. E)
ENGAGE IN NONTHREATENING GAMES

■ Prompt children to interface with the dog in safe, nonthreatening games. Toy accessories are especially useful here (Fig. E).

■ Do not let children interface with the dog while it is eating or sleeping.

■ Children should postpone aggressive hugging until the dog knows them well. Many canines find this behavior threatening.

■ Children should postpone rough play until the dog knows them well and its personality (and propensity for aggressive action) is well understood.

■ Do not allow children to tug on the dog's ears and/or tail. These are highly sensitive areas for the canine.

■ Any dog who will spend time with children should receive thorough obedience and socialization training.

⚠ *CAUTION: Very young children should never, under any circumstances, be left alone with a dog—even a dog that knows them and has shown no aggressive tendencies.*

Interfacing with Other Dogs

Introducing a new dog into a home that already contains one can be challenging. Canines must establish a "pecking order," with the most dominant animal becoming pack leader. If you bring a second or third dog into your home, this is the first issue the dogs will resolve. The key is to make sure it happens with minimal discord. Under close human supervision, this difficult but necessary aspect of canine behavior can be accommodated with minimal fuss.

[1] When you bring the new dog into your home, make sure your current pet is confined to a specific section of the house, out of sight.

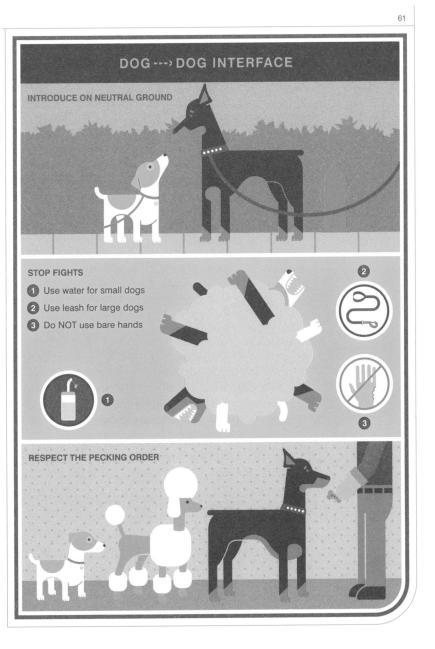

[2] Allow the new model to roam the house for several hours. The new model will scent the current dog and become aware that it is not alone.

[3] Introduce the two dogs—not in your home but on neutral ground. Try the sidewalk in front of your house. This will eliminate issues of territorial defense. Both animals should be leashed. If the dogs are large, enlist another person to help.

[4] If the dogs appear to tolerate each other, take them both back to the house. However, do not leave them alone together. It can take weeks or even months for the dogs to develop a healthy relationship; until that happens, they should interact only under your direct supervision.

[5] If the dogs do not tolerate each other, try briefly crating the new dog and giving your current model the run of the house. Then briefly crate the current model and let the new dog out. After they become more familiar with each other, release both dogs and allow them to interact under your supervision.

[6] If the dogs fight, do not try to separate them with your hands. For smaller dogs, use a squeeze bottle of water to temporarily distract both canines. Larger dogs should be equipped with leashes, so they can be pulled apart.

[7] Give each dog separate food and water bowls, separate beds, and separate crates. Sharing such personal effects may lead to strife.

[8] Once your dogs establish a pecking order, respect it. Greet the pack leader first when you come home (it will be obvious who the pack leader is). This dog should also be fed first and should receive preferred access

to treats and attention. Ignoring the pecking order may cause the dogs to become confused or agitated.

⚠ **EXPERT TIP:** *A puppy will almost invariably submit to an older dog, even if the puppy is a Great Dane and the older dog is a Chihuahua. However, if the older dog is appreciably larger, do not let it attack or excessively bully the newcomer.*

Interfacing with Cats

The idea that dogs are hardwired to vex cats is not true. However, many dogs are programmed to chase small prey, which cats, unfortunately, resemble. Before interfacing your canine with a feline, be sure you understand the extent of your dog's "prey drive." For instance, a Shih Tzu will exhibit little or none, while hunters such as greyhounds (bred for the chase) and terriers (bred to fight and kill small game) may display quite a bit. To gauge the dog's prey drive, simply toss a favorite toy across the room. The dog may ignore it (low), pick it up and return it to you (medium), or aggressively chase it down, then shake and chew it (high). This does not necessarily mean the dog will try to kill your cat, but it may very much want to harass it.

Problems can be prevented by following these rules of introduction.

[1] When the new dog is first introduced to the home, confine your cat(s) to another section of the house. Allow the dog to orient itself and become less agitated.

[2] Once the dog has become acclimated, direct its attention to the (closed) door, behind which the cat resides. Allow the animals to sniff and perhaps touch each other under the door (Fig. A).

(Fig. A)
UNDER-THE-DOOR INTRODUCTION

(Fig. B)
ALLOW ESCAPE AREA FOR FELINE WITH:

1 Food and water bowls

2 Litter box

FLUFFY

DOG ---> CAT INTERFACE: Some dogs are hardwired to chase small prey,

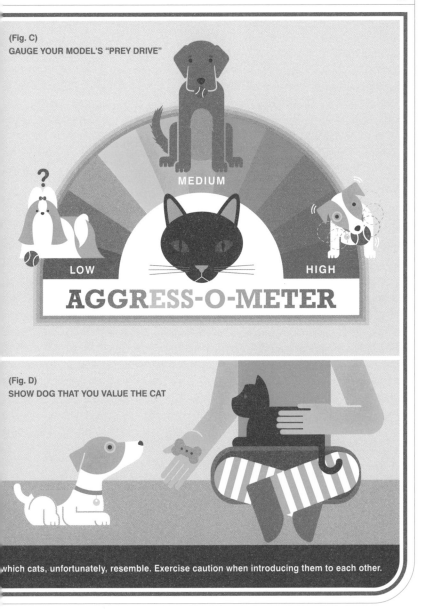

(Fig. C)
GAUGE YOUR MODEL'S "PREY DRIVE"

MEDIUM

?

LOW   HIGH

AGGRESS-O-METER

(Fig. D)
SHOW DOG THAT YOU VALUE THE CAT

which cats, unfortunately, resemble. Exercise caution when introducing them to each other.

[3] Introduce the two under close supervision. The dog should be leashed. Alternatively, you could crate the dog and release the cat.

[4] During these early encounters, offer the dog special treats or extra attention whenever the cat appears. This programs the canine to associate the cat with positive things.

[5] Give the cat a high shelf or gated room where it can retreat from the dog if it wishes (Fig. B).

[6] Stroke and hold the cat in the dog's presence. The dog will sense that you value the other animal (Fig. D).

[7] Place the cat's litter box someplace inaccessible to the dog. Canines like to eat cat feces, an action that could result in malfunction.

[8] Provide two sets of food bowls, water bowls, and beds in separate locations. The cat and the dog should each have its own sanctuary for eating and resting.

⚠ **EXPERT TIP:** *It is not uncommon for cats to try to harass dogs. However, in most cases the dog can (and will) end the problem with a few loud barks.*

First Night at Home

Whatever sleeping arrangement you select for your dog, make sure its components are already in place when the animal arrives. In most cases a puppy should (for the first few nights at least) be allowed to sleep near your bed. This is for your convenience as well the canine's. The puppy will

probably whimper during the night, so comforting it will be as simple as reaching over the side of the mattress. However, do not allow the puppy to sleep with you; this creates a precedent that can be hard to change.

The puppy may be comforted by the presence of a hot-water bottle, a ticking alarm clock, or a softly playing radio. The puppy should not have unlimited access to the house at night. Move its crate into the bedroom, or close your bedroom door, or install a child gate to deter unauthorized elimination or chewing incidents. Make sure the puppy has toilet arrangements, such as a spread of newspapers, nearby. Be prepared for accidents—and to be awakened during the first few nights by whimpering. (See "Crate Training," page 81.)

Selecting a Name

Picking a name for your dog is a highly personal decision. However, a few rules may guide you in your quest.

■ Dogs have an easier time identifying a multisyllabic rather than a mono-syllabic name. Consequently, Rover is better than Spot.

■ Use the dog's name often. Repeat it while petting, holding, or playing with it.

■ Do not use the dog's name with an angry tone or when disciplining it.

■ Make sure the dog's name doesn't sound like a commonly used command word. For instance, "Ray" and "stay."

■ If an adult dog has already been assigned a name, keep it. While "Bon Jovi" might not have been *your* first choice, trying to alter it will only add to your pet's adjustment issues.

⚠ *EXPERT TIP: Owners who bestow human names on their canines (Jenny, Ben, etc.) tend to hold their dogs in higher regard.*

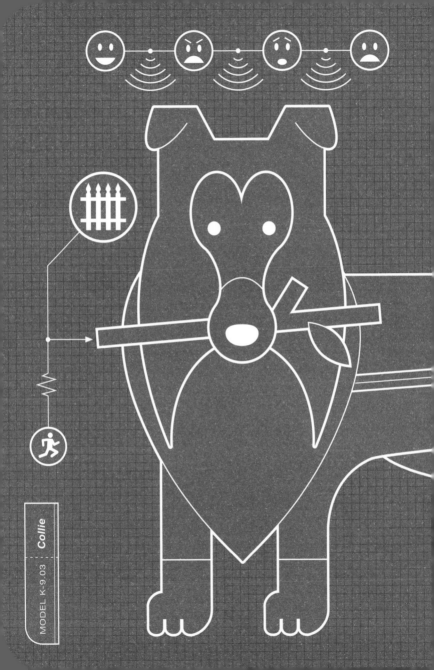

MODEL K-9.03 _ Collie

Chapter 3

Daily Interaction

Audio Cues and Body Language

Audible dog communication typically assumes one of the following forms:

Howls: Wolves howl to locate other pack members over long distances. Many domestic dogs have kept this behavior. It can sometimes be initiated by such things as police sirens.

Growls: This sound is often associated with aggression, threats, and displays of dominance. However, dogs may growl during play as well. Study the dog's body language to distinguish one from the other.

Grunts: These are often heard when dogs greet humans or other dogs. They are the equivalent of a human sigh.

Whines: A form of communication over intermediate ranges that can signal anything from pain to submission to happiness at meeting someone.

Barks: As with howling, these can be used to get attention, to raise the alarm, or to identify an individual. A dog who is anxious tends to bark in a high pitch; a dog who is warning off an intruder barks at a lower pitch. Warning barks may become more rapid as a stranger gets closer.

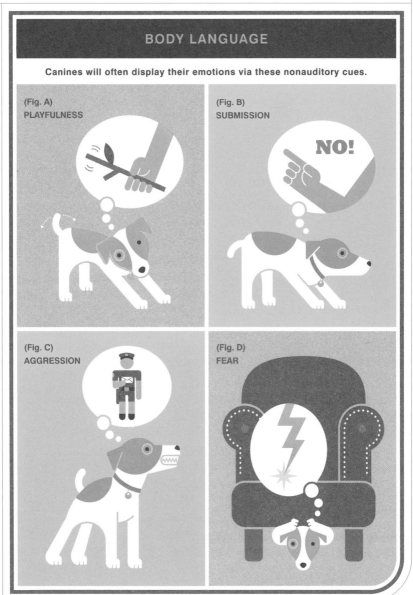

Dogs and Human Speech

Dogs do not "understand" human speech at all. However, they can associate audio cues (words) with the execution of various behaviors. For instance, though a collie does not comprehend that "stay" is a word, it does understand that this particular sound calls for a specific behavior. Some dogs can store dozens of words or other audio cues this way. In fact, the word itself may not be as important as how you say it. Dogs can gauge your mood by the tone of your voice, so saying something—anything—with an angry tone will usually elicit a fearful or submissive response. Likewise, saying "bad dog" in a cheerful voice will not achieve the desired effect.

Sleep Mode

Dogs sleep roughly 14 hours a day. Older or larger dogs (such as Saint Bernards or Newfoundlands) will sleep even more. Instead of sleeping in one continuous stretch—as most humans do—dogs will take naps of varying lengths throughout the day.

Canine sleep patterns mirror those of humans. When a canine first goes to sleep it enters a "quiet" phase, followed shortly thereafter by "active" or REM (rapid eye movement) sleep. The dog's eyes move under its eyelids, its legs jerk, and it may whine or softly bark. There is no way to know with certainty (because they have no way to tell their owners), but the dog gives every impression of dreaming.

EXPERT TIP: If your dog has trouble sleeping through the night, consider increasing its play/exercise time.

Dog Identification Methods

Your dog should wear its collar, with identification tags attached, at all times. The tag should include your name, address, and home and work telephone numbers. The dog's rabies vaccination and license tags (stamped with your veterinarian's name and telephone number) should also be attached. In many towns and cities, this is mandatory. Dogs can also be tattooed or fitted with an identification microchip (the veterinarian-preferred method for permanent identification). About the size of a grain of rice, the microchip is injected just under the skin between the shoulder blades. When scanned, it produces information that can assist the dog's finder in locating its owner. Chip scanners are used at all lost-dog intake locations, including humane societies, city pounds, and veterinary hospitals. However, a "chipped" dog still needs to wear a collar with identification.

EXPERT TIP: *If you travel with your dog on vacation, update its tags by including your temporary phone number.*

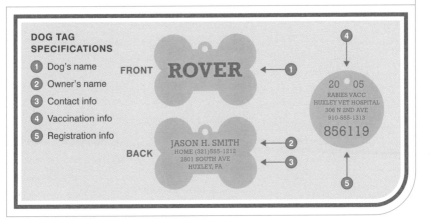

Exercise and Fitness

Even the most sedentary models require a certain amount of physical exertion to stay healthy. Consider the following factors before determining the level of exercise appropriate for your pet.

Size: For small breeds such as pugs and Boston terriers, a walk around the block is the equivalent of a marathon. Larger animals are, in general, capable of longer jaunts and more strenuous activity.

Physical Stamina: How long and how hard a dog can play depends on its genetic makeup. Some models, including huskies and most terriers, were bred for stamina. They can run and play for a very, very long time. Others were designed for specific types of exertion. For instance, the greyhound is capable of great speed, but only over short distances. As a result, it makes a poor jogging companion. Models such as the German shorthaired pointer and the vizsla, however, were engineered to go the distance.

Physical Makeup: Various breeds, because of their design, have certain physiological disadvantages. For instance, "flat-faced" models such as boxers, pugs, and bulldogs have below-normal breathing capacity and therefore less stamina. Physical activity for these dogs should come in short bursts. Also, some models are prone to orthopedic problems (such as hip dysplasia) that can be aggravated by excessive exercise. Your veterinarian can help you create a suitable exercise plan for your dog.

Weather Conditions: Coat length also can determine how much exercise a particular model can handle. In winter, thin-coated dogs can tolerate less cold exposure than thick-coated dogs such as the Samoyed and Great Pyrenees. During the summer months, however, thin-coated dogs can tolerate more heat than heavily coated breeds. In general, heat is a bigger problem for most dogs.

⚠️ **CAUTION:** *Be extremely careful with "flat-faced" breeds (bulldogs, pugs) during times of high heat and humidity. Their inability to dissipate heat during otherwise normal exertion can be potentially life-threatening.*

Physical Conditioning: Dogs, like humans, can become out of shape. Taking a normally sedentary dog on a 2-mile run can lead to orthopedic injuries (among other problems). Instead, build up the dog's capacity slowly over weeks and exercise it daily, if possible. A sedentary dog can be conditioned with a 20- to 60-minute walk 5 days a week. Swimming is also a good activity, because it eases strain on joints. Consult your veterinarian before beginning any sort of exercise program for an overweight, aged, and/or infirm canine.

⚠️ **CAUTION:** *A dog, in attempting to please its owner, may persist in a physical activity beyond the point of exhaustion, putting it in danger of mechanical damage. Monitor your dog's physical regimen and discontinue it at the first sign of serious fatigue.*

How to Teach "Fetch"

Fetch is a great all-purpose exercise. However, it is important to remember that not all dogs are programmed to play this game. Some breeds are not very "reactive"—that is, attuned to the sorts of quick movements a ball, stick, or Frisbee makes. But terriers, herding dogs, and retrievers often love the game. In such cases teaching can be simple. First toss the object (Fig. A). After the dog chases it down and collects

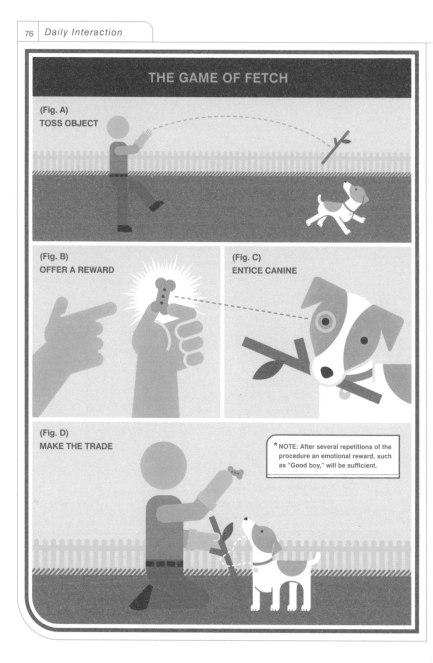

it, offer a treat (Fig. B) to entice the canine back to you (Fig. C). Give up the treat after the dog releases the object into your hand (Fig. D). Repeat until the dog understands what is expected. Soon you can offer praise (and another toss) as a reward, rather than food.

Yard Containment Protocol

If possible, dogs should have a secure outdoor area in which to exercise and/or download wastes. Containment options include the following.

Fencing: The standard method. Be sure the dog cannot crawl or tunnel under the enclosure. Also, be sure exterior access gates can be locked, to prevent unauthorized entry.

Invisible Fences: These "fences" are in fact electric lines buried around the perimeter of the dog owner's property. When the dog approaches the line, its collar sounds a warning signal, then delivers an uncomfortable electric shock if the canine continues forward. Dogs cannot dig their way under the system as they can with conventional fencing. However, a large or excited dog can escape simply by ignoring the shock. Also, nothing prevents unauthorized people and/or pets from entering your yard.

Chain: Should only be used when your dog is being let out to relieve himself—and only if your yard is not adequately fenced. Leaving a dog on a chain for any length of time is inhumane.

Dog Run: A small portion of the yard that is fenced and may contain a doghouse. Again, your model should not be confined for any length of time to a dog run. Because the area is small, it must be cleaned frequently.

① FENCING

② CHAIN

TINY

YARD CONTAINMENT PROTOCOL: The type of outdoor containment you

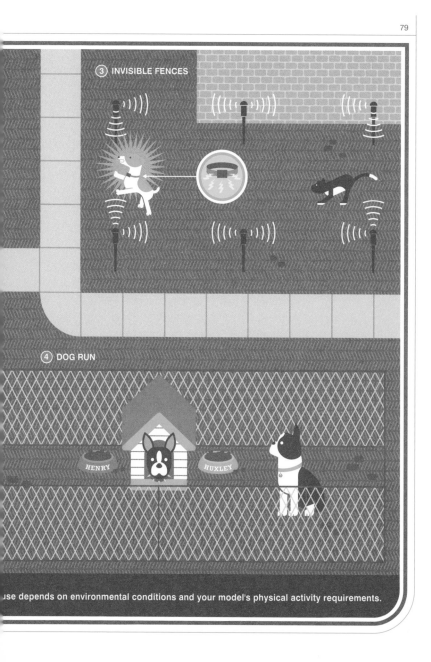

③ INVISIBLE FENCES

④ DOG RUN

HENRY

HUXLEY

use depends on environmental conditions and your model's physical activity requirements.

⚠ **CAUTION:** *If your dog is accustomed to being indoors, do not leave it outdoors and unattended for long periods of time. Such animals may develop severe emotional problems, become excessively dirty, and/or injure themselves.*

Outdoor Storage

Many dog models are suitable for outdoor storage, as long as they receive the necessary support equipment: a storage facility or "house" that is raised off the ground and large enough for the animal to turn around in easily. It should be located in a shaded area inside a contained space (fenced yard or dog run) and be equipped with hay or other bedding during winter. Water should always be available and frequently changed.

Be advised, however, that many experts believe prolonged outdoor storage can degrade a dog's performance. Canines want to be with their pack (in this case, you and your family), so confining them outdoors can be viewed by dogs as punishment. Also, outdoor dogs, because they receive less time with humans, tend to be less socialized. With proper training and attention to hygiene, even the largest breeds can be kept indoors.

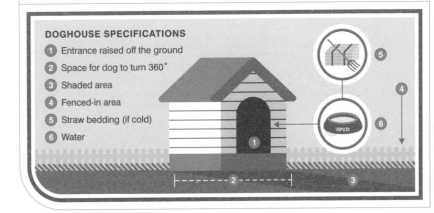

DOGHOUSE SPECIFICATIONS

1. Entrance raised off the ground
2. Space for dog to turn 360°
3. Shaded area
4. Fenced-in area
5. Straw bedding (if cold)
6. Water

Waste Disposal Protocols

Though dogs are usually considered to be "earth friendly" products, own-ers should remember that they can emit prodigious quantities of toxic waste. The following section outlines how to safely manage this problem.

Crate Training

This is a popular puppy house-training method that, when used prop-erly, teaches a young canine where and when to relieve itself. It also provides the animal with a safe and secure retreat—a retreat that can be moved anywhere the owner desires. The method works because dogs are hardwired to not soil the place where they sleep. When exe-cuted correctly, this technique programs the puppy to "hold it" until it is allowed to go outside.

⚠ *CAUTION: Crate training is not a long-term storage method. Puppies should not be left alone for extended periods in their crates. If the dog ever soils the crate, this can set back house-training by weeks.*

[1] Purchase a dog crate equipped with metal bars or a high-impact plastic body and metal grate. Be sure the crate is large enough for the dog to turn around in—but not too large. It should be used as a sleeping area, not a playpen.

[2] Line the crate with a blanket or soft towel. Add a couple of toys.

[3] Encourage the puppy to expel its waste before entering the crate.

[4] Place the puppy in the crate for a short period of time. Provide a

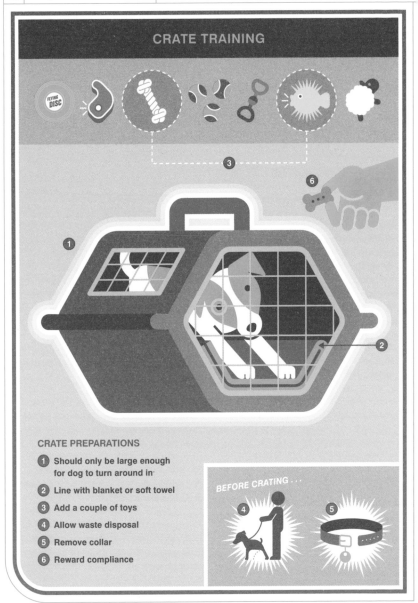

CRATE TRAINING

CRATE PREPARATIONS

1. Should only be large enough for dog to turn around in
2. Line with blanket or soft towel
3. Add a couple of toys
4. Allow waste disposal
5. Remove collar
6. Reward compliance

BEFORE CRATING . . .

small treat, so the puppy associates its confinement with good things. Stay nearby until the puppy settles down. Removing the puppy's collar will prevent it from getting snagged on any part of the crate.

[5] Never release the puppy when it barks. Wait until it stops barking before releasing.

[6] Begin placing the puppy in the crate for its naps and other downtimes. During the day, you should never leave the puppy in the crate for more than 4 hours at a time.

⚠ **EXPERT TIP:** *A good rule of thumb is that the maximum number of hours a dog should remain in the crate is its age in months plus one. For instance, a 2-month-old puppy should never be crated more than 3 hours without (at least) a bathroom break.*

[7] The puppy should sleep in the crate during the night. Be aware that it will probably require at least one bathroom break midway through the night.

[8] After your puppy is released from the crate, immediately offer it the opportunity to expel its waste. If it does, praise the puppy and allow it to roam the house freely for a while. If not, return the puppy to the crate for 10 to 15 minutes. Then try again.

⚠ **EXPERT TIP:** *Give the puppy plenty of opportunities to relieve itself. It should have a "bathroom break" first thing in the morning; after every meal; after every nap; after strenuous play sessions; last thing at night; and during the night if it appears restless. When escorting the puppy outside, always take it out the same door and to the same spot.*

[9] Puppies can be weaned from the crate at 5 or 6 months of age, after earning the owner's trust. However, the crate can always remain their "home." This will make transportation easy, because you can take their safe, secure environment anywhere you go.

House-Training

Even newly adopted adult dogs may require a "refresher course" on waste management. When you sense that the dog is ready to use the bathroom, quickly escort it outside to a spot you would like it to use (Fig. A). You might want to leash the dog to keep it from straying. If it uses the spot, praise it strongly and perhaps offer a treat. Afterward, keep a sharp eye on the dog and take it to the spot whenever it seems in need of relief. Regularly clear away feces. In no time the dog should start visiting the spot on its own—and requesting bathroom breaks when needed.

Dealing with Unauthorized Downloads

It is important to thoroughly clean up urine puddles in the house, because dogs tend to return to and reuse spots they have targeted earlier. Several commercial products remove stains and kill lingering odors. A homemade mix of 50 percent white vinegar and 50 percent water (Fig. B) will remove urine smells (but not the odor of feces).

EXPERT TIP: Do not admonish a dog (especially a puppy) if it urinates in the house (Fig. C). Negative reinforcement does not work with housebreaking. Unless you act while the dog is literally in the middle of soiling the carpet (Fig D), it will not associate the punishment with the unauthorized urination. Remember that accidents are often the result of inattentiveness by the owner.

Chapter 4

Basic Programming

Overview of Factory-Installed Software

The dog comes with a great deal of pre-installed programming. Though its operating system is more or less the same one used by its wild cousin, the wolf, the software has been altered in important ways to make the dog more amenable to life with humans. Here are some of the key points.

Socialization: Because they were designed to live in groups, dogs are highly attuned to the moods of their pack mates—in this case, you and your family. That's why it is ideal for puppies to join their new families during the seventh or eighth week of life. This is the period in which they are most susceptible to imprinting.

Dominance: Dog packs are structured around a well-established pecking order, from the leader, or alpha, on down. To enjoy the maximum benefits of this software, you must establish yourself as the dog's alpha. (See "Establishing Dominance," next page.)

Hunting: This key aspect of wolf behavior has been altered in many important ways. In herding breeds, the urge to actually kill game has been suppressed, while the drive to stalk it has been accentuated. Many dog behaviors (nipping at heels, chasing tossed objects) are related to hunting.

Territoriality: Dogs are programmed to stake out and defend territory. In most cases this will be your house and (often) the yard. Canines who might be quite mild if they met a stranger on neutral territory can be highly aggressive if they encounter the same person or animal on their home terrain.

Territorial Marking: Dogs, like wolves, mark the limits of their domain with urine and feces. This behavior greatly eases the process of housebreaking. Since dogs will repeatedly mark the same spots, pick a location in the yard where you want your pet to expel its waste. After the dog has used the spot a few times, it will update its internal preferences and remember the spot forever.

Establishing Dominance

If you acquire a dog as a puppy, it will in most cases automatically—and forevermore—see you as its superior. As for adult dogs, the simple act of providing their food strongly reinforces your primacy. Also, dogs that are markedly smaller than you will usually accept your authority. However, some particularly high-spirited breeds (Jack Russells, Dobermans, Akitas) may choose, on occasion, to challenge. This can manifest itself in interesting ways: The dog may growl or snap if you try to move it off your bed; aggressively defend its food bowl; or even refuse to give you "right of way" when you pass. Such problems must be dealt with promptly, before they escalate into more serious challenges.

Troubleshooting Dominance Issues

■ If a dog is having trouble with one member of its human family, have that person start feeding the animal. When the canine sees where its food comes from, it will often submit to the provider.

■ A dog that stands on its hind legs, puts its forepaws on your chest or shoulders and looks you in the eye is trying to dominate you. Do not allow this behavior.

■ If a dog wants a treat or a toy, make it perform some trick or obey a command before providing it. This reinforces the chain of authority.

■ One of the perks of being the dominant pack member is "right of way"—

A:/SOCIALIZATION

B:/DOMINANCE

FACTORY-INSTALLED SOFTWARE: The dog includes numerous

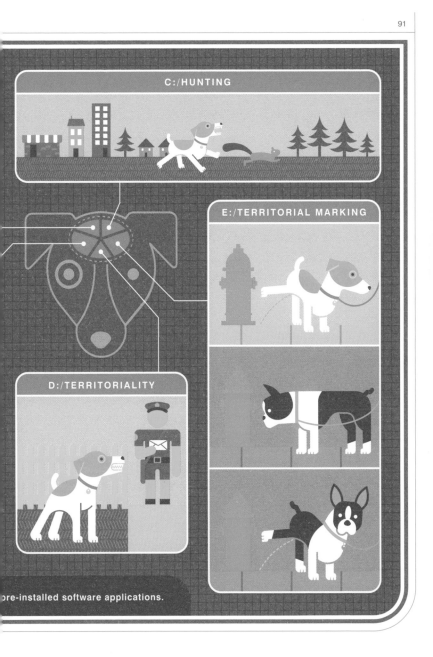

C:/HUNTING

E:/TERRITORIAL MARKING

D:/TERRITORIALITY

pre-installed software applications.

animals with lower status must get out of your path. For this reason, if your dog is in your way, do not move. Make it move.

■ If your dog seems to develop dominance issues with a child, seek the help of a veterinarian and/or a professional trainer immediately.

Training Options (Software Add-ons)

While the home enthusiast can install the following software options himself, less-knowledgeable dog owners should consider attending an obedience class.

Socialization

Puppies should learn how to meet new people and pets without display-ing fear or aggression. One of the best ways to accomplish this is to introduce the puppy to many people. These sessions should be calm, brief experiences in which the puppy is handled and petted, but allowed to retreat if it tires of the encounter. Supervised sessions with other dogs are also a good idea—but only after the puppy has received its full set of vaccinations. The puppy can also participate in a socialization class, where it will meet other canines and people under controlled conditions.

Leash Training

A puppy can be introduced to a leash long before it is mature enough to attempt a proper "walk." Attach a small, lightweight version to the puppy's collar and allow it to walk around the yard (supervised) as the leash trails behind it. Later you can pick up the leash and nonchalantly "walk" the canine. Trying to guide the animal is unnecessary; you just want it to become familiar with the leash.

Once the dog has received its full set of vaccinations (see Chapter 8), it will be ready to undertake a proper walk. Bring the dog to an open space that is free from distractions (such as other dogs, children, and/or wild game). Place the dog on a leash and begin walking. Whenever the dog begins to pull, stop walking. Wait until the dog stops pulling, then offer praise and resume the walk.

Repeat the process for as many training sessions as necessary. It is acceptable to sternly say "no" if your puppy pulls constantly. However, patient, consistent handling is the real key to effective leash management.

EXPERT TIP: *Obedience sessions should take place twice a day, but each should last no more than 5 or 10 minutes. If they take too long, the dog may become bored.*

CAUTION: *"Choke" and "pinch" collars are unnecessary for leash training. They can even be harmful to smaller breeds. Should your dog pull excessively, consider a halter-type lead. This device places pressure on the dog's shoulders instead of its throat.*

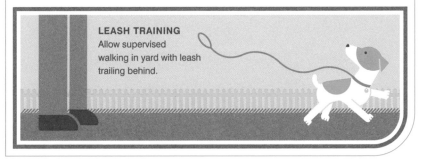

LEASH TRAINING
Allow supervised walking in yard with leash trailing behind.

Sit

[1] Begin training indoors. The room should be free of distractions.

[2] Summon the dog, then show it a treat. Hold the treat so that the dog points its nose upward (Fig. A). Move the treat backward over its head until the dog naturally lowers into a sitting position (Fig. B).

[3] As soon as it sits, give it the treat and offer ample praise.

[4] Repeat the exercise, this time saying "sit."

[5] Once the dog learns the command, try it in more distracting settings: the yard, on a sidewalk, and so on.

Stay

[1] Command the dog to sit.

[2] Once it assumes the position, say "stay" (Fig. C), then wait 2 seconds before praising and/or giving a reward. Be sure the dog holds the sit position during this time. Repeat as many times as necessary.

[3] Once it masters this step, tell it to stay, then take several steps back as the dog holds its position (Fig. D). Wait 2 seconds before rewarding dog.

[4] As the dog becomes more competent, add further distractions such as running in place or making odd noises (Fig. E). Also, increase the interval between the command and the reward. Do not move on to the next step until your dog complies with these new demands.

[5] Gradually increase the length of time the dog stays and the distance you move from it.

[6] Pick a word or phrase, such as "free time," to let the dog know when it no longer has to stay. It should hold its position until it hears that phrase.

Heel

This important leash-walking protocol teaches the dog to walk by your knee, matching your pace and ignoring distractions.

[1] Hold the dog's leash in your right hand, taking up any slack with your left. The dog should stand at your left side.

[2] Command the dog to sit (Fig. A).

[3] While holding a treat in your left hand, bring it to the dog's nose and say its name, followed by "heel" (Fig. B).

[4] Walk for a short distance, keeping the food at your side (Fig. C).

[5] When you stop, say the dog's name, followed by the word "heel," and raise the treat so the dog sits (Fig. D).

[6] Give the dog its reward, then repeat the process until the dog walks faultlessly at your side, whether wearing a leash or not.

⚠ *CAUTION: Heel training is not a substitute for a leash, which should still be used in all public situations.*

Coming When Called

[1] Solicit help from a friend or family member. Each person should sit at opposite ends of a room. Take turns calling the canine from one person to the other, saying "come" in a pleasant, enthusiastic voice (Fig. A).

[2] Bribe the dog with treats and/or praise to win compliance. Make the idea of coming when called as attractive as possible.

[3] Later that day, call the dog at random times, whether the animal is a few feet away or in another room. Reward it amply when it responds.

[4] When the dog consistently comes the first time it is called, put it on a long leash and move the training outside (Fig. B). Take the dog for a walk, allowing it to put a fair distance between itself and you (but always on a leash). Ask it to come, and if it complies reward it with treats and praise. If it doesn't, tug firmly on the leash and pull, still calling to it in a friendly voice. When it finally returns to you, reward the dog lavishly. Repeat the process several times.

[5] Once the dog is competently trained, upgrade to a longer leash and repeat step 4.

[6] Next, practice off the leash in a fenced area (Fig. C). If your dog refuses to come when called, do not keep calling. Sit down on the ground or do something unusual (but nonthreatening) that it will want to investigate. When it returns, put the leash on. Go back to leash training for several days before attempting another leash-free session. Eventually the dog will catch on.

[7] Saying "come" should always be associated in the canine's mind with pleasant things. Never call a dog to punish it. Instead, go to the

canine. If the animal associates the word "come" with punishment, it may not respond.

Training Tips

■ If a dog exhibits an undesirable behavior, the best approach is to pointedly ignore the behavior and the animal. The dog will quickly realize that doing the wrong thing deprives it of what it desires most—attention. The only exception is when a dog becomes extremely aggressive; this type of undesirable behavior requires your immediate attention. (See "Establishing Dominance," page 89.)

■ Shouting at a dog when it does something wrong can have unintended consequences. Canines are programmed to crave attention—positive or negative. If one of their transgressions leads to an uproar, they may be tempted to repeat it.

■ Do not reprimand a dog for a transgression unless you catch the animal in the act of committing it. A dog will not understand that you are angry about something it did an hour ago. It will simply know that you are angry—perhaps about what it is doing at that moment.

■ Never strike or harshly reprimand a puppy or adult dog. This is always counterproductive because it teaches the canine, first and foremost, to fear you. In the case of guarding breeds with high levels of innate aggression, it can also be very dangerous.

■ Always end teaching sessions on a high note. If a dog is having trouble with a new lesson, have it finish by doing an already-mastered behavior that it can successfully execute. Praise it lavishly.

■ Hold instruction sessions at the same times and places each day.

■ Try to use command words such as "sit" with the same tone of voice each time. Dogs respond as much to *how* you say things as *what* you say.

■ Be sure you have the dog's attention before giving a command.

Selecting an Obedience Program

Most veterinarians can suggest qualified obedience programs in your area. These usually meet once a week over several weeks and cover such basics as socialization, walking on a leash, and simple commands. Understand, however, that attending a class does not free you from the responsibility of training your canine. The class will merely demonstrate techniques. You will still have to spend many hours applying them to your pet.

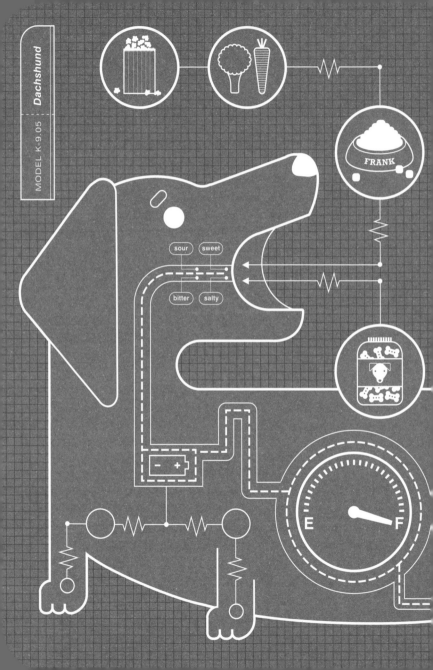

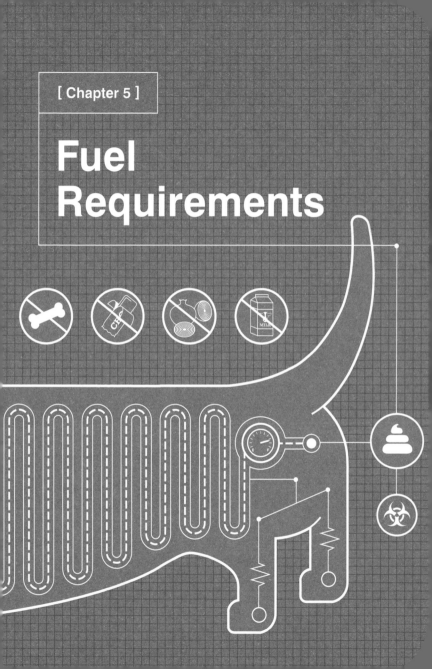

[Chapter 5]

Fuel
Requirements

Types of Fuel

Dog foods are divided into broad categories—dry and canned. Dry is the most popular. It contains more nutrition by weight, is less expensive than canned, and its hardness may help reduce dental tartar. Canned food is favored by dogs themselves and includes fewer calories by volume (it is approximately 70 percent water).

Special foods are available to counter everything from diabetes to obesity to allergies. Lamb is often the centerpiece of such formulations because very few canines are allergic to it. Aging dogs may also have special dietary needs. Their kidneys handle protein less efficiently, sometimes necessitating a low-protein food. The onset of heart disease, liver and/or kidney difficulties, stomach problems, and other concerns can also call for special diets.

When feeding a commercially produced food, begin by offering your dog the recommended daily serving. Be prepared to alter this, however, because recommended portions tend to be slightly more than what dogs actually require to maintain their weight. Never give "high protein" or "puppy formula" foods to dogs more than a year old.

EXPERT TIP: Unless you are prepared to work very hard at it, do not try to make your dog's food. Creating the proper balance of nutrients, minerals, and vitamins takes a great deal of effort.

Fuel Facts

Nutritional needs vary from canine to canine and hinge on such things as size, activity level, and age.

■ Small dogs need more calories per pound of body mass than larger dogs.
■ A very sedentary dog may need 30 percent fewer calories than an average dog of the same size.

- Very active dogs may require 40 to 50 percent more calories than an average dog.
- Pregnant or lactating dogs may need 30 to 50 percent more calories than usual—sometimes even double their normal serving.
- During winter, dogs who spend time outside may need additional food, because maintaining a constant body temperature requires more calories.

Approximate Daily Fuel Requirements

	DAILY CALORIC INTAKE	
Weight	Puppies	Adult Dogs
- 5 pounds/2 kg	- 500	- 250
- 10 pounds/4.5 kg	- 850	- 450
- 20 pounds/9 kg	- 1400	- 700
- 30 pounds/13.5 kg	- 1800	- 900
- 40 pounds/18 kg	- 2300	- 1200
- 50 pounds/22.5 kg	- 2700	- 1400
- 60 pounds/27 kg	- 3200	- 1600
- 70 pounds/31.5 kg	- 3600	- 1500
- 80 pounds/36 kg	——	- 1800
- 90 pounds/40.5 kg	——	- 2100
- 100 pounds/45 kg	——	- 2300

Selecting a Brand

The makers of dog food, just like the makers of processed human foods, are required by law to post nutritional information on their labels. Such labels must list, among other things, the ingredients and a statement of nutritional purpose and adequacy (basically, an explanation as to what sort of dog the food is meant for).

Examine the statement of nutritional purpose and adequacy first. For instance, a product formulated for puppies and pregnant females might read, "Complete and balanced nutrition for growth and reproduction." Or a food for adult canines might say, "Complete and balanced nutrition for growth and maintenance of adult dogs." Top products will state that these claims are based on "Association of American Feed Control Officials (AAFCO) feeding protocols." Lesser products may base their assertions solely on a nutrient analysis that "meets AAFCO nutrient profile recommendations." In short, the higher-quality product was subjected to a feeding study; the lesser product only to a lab test.

After selecting a balanced, nutritionally complete product that is designed to meet your dog's needs, examine the ingredients. The heaviest ingredient by weight is listed first. Wet foods will almost always list a meat product first, while in dry preparations meat may appear farther down the roster. This is because in wet foods the meat is hydrated and therefore heavier. Dry products may contain just as much meat, but because it weighs less it sits slightly lower on the ingredient list.

In general, some form of meat should be near the top of any list. Meat by-products (these can range from bonemeal to poultry feathers) are generally of a lower quality. Cereals and soy are also important ingredients and should appear prominently. Plant hulls are low-quality foods, but may be added to increase fiber. Vitamins, minerals, and preservatives, used in minute amounts, will appear last on any ingredients list.

If you wish to compare brands, examine the guaranteed analysis printed on the container. This explains what percentage of the product is made up of protein, fat, fiber, and moisture. To make such comparisons meaningful, ask your veterinarian what percentages are right for your dog.

How to Feed

Do not "free feed"—that is, leave a bowl of food sitting out all day so that the canine can serve itself. This may lead to obesity. Pick a time to offer a meal, present the food, then, after perhaps half an hour, put away the bowl until the next feeding. Twice-daily feedings (once in the morning, once in the evening) will suffice for most models.

Puppies up to 12 weeks of age should receive three meals a day and twice-daily feedings thereafter. Small-breed puppies may need more frequent feedings to avoid hypoglycemia. At 9 to 12 months puppies should be switched to adult food and less-frequent feedings. Nutritional supplements not recommended by a veterinarian should be avoided; too much protein and/or calcium can cause joint and skeletal problems. For more information on puppy nutrition, see page 141.

Modifying Diet

Suddenly switching a dog's food can lead to stomach upset and diarrhea. To avoid this, change the product gradually. On the first day, mix three parts of the current food with one part of the new food. On the next day, mix them evenly. On the third day, offer three-fourths new food. Then switch entirely to the new product.

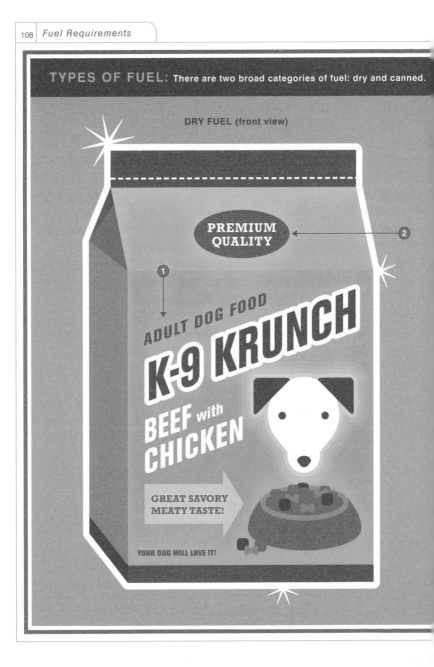

Examine the nutritional purpose and ingredients carefully before selecting a brand.

DRY FUEL (side view)

CANNED FUEL (front view)

1

2

PREMIUM QUALITY

K-9 DeLITE

BEEF with LAMB

DIET DOG FOOD

1

Complete and balanced nutrition for growth and maintenance of adult dogs.

2 Based on AAFCO feeding protocols

Ingredients: Chicken, Chicken Broth, Beef, Wheat Grass Powder, Soy, Carrots, Broccoli, Cabbage, Peas, Ground Flax, Poultry Feathers, Vitamin A Supplement, Niacin Supplement, and Vitamin B12 Supplement

3

4

5

1 Complete and balanced nutrition for growth and maintenance of overweight dogs

2 Based on AAFCO feeding protocols

Ingredients: Beef, Lamb Broth, Liver, Wheat Grass Powder, Soy, Broccoli, Peas, Bonemeal, Vitamin A Supplement, and Niacin Supplement

3

4

5

CANNED FUEL (back view)

1 Nutritional purpose and adequacy statement

2 Indicates a high quality product was subjected to a feeding study instead of only a lab test

The order in which the ingredients are listed is determined by weight (heaviest is listed first)

3 Meat should be near the top of the list

4 Cereals and soy should be listed prominently

5 Vitamins, minerals, and preservatives should appear last, as they are used minutely

FUEL SUPPLEMENTS

NUTRITIOUS SNACKS

1. Low-calorie dog treats
2. Air-popped popcorn (no salt or butter)
3. Broccoli
4. Cooked green beans
5. Raw carrots

HAZARDOUS MATERIALS

1. Table scraps
2. Bones
3. Cat food
4. Chocolate
5. Onions
6. Milk

Fuel Supplements (Snacks)

Snacks should compose no more than 10 percent of a dog's daily caloric intake. Appropriate snacks include:

- Commercial low-calorie dog treats
- Air-popped popcorn without butter or salt
- Broccoli
- Cooked green beans
- Raw carrots

The following snacks are unhealthy and possibly even fatal to dogs:

- Table scraps (they are usually too fatty and not attuned to a dog's nutritional needs; if you must provide them, do so sparingly).
- Bones (small ones can become caught in the airway; large ones may splinter and can cause any number of problems, from choking to intestinal blockage to internal punctures).
- Cat food (dogs love it, but it is not formulated to meet their nutritional needs).
- Chocolate (toxic to canines, small amounts of chocolate can make dogs sick; large amounts can be fatal).
- Onions (consumption of too many onions will cause the dog's red blood cells to burst, triggering anemia).
- Milk (dogs, like most adult mammals, often suffer from lactose intolerance; a large dose of milk can trigger intestinal distress and diarrhea).

Gas Emissions

Most canines will, from time to time, suffer from excess methane discharges. There are several ways to handle such exhaust problems.

- Give the dog activated charcoal tablets, which will absorb the excess gas.
- Overeating can cause gas, so try serving smaller portions in more feedings.
- Dogs who eat too fast may swallow too much air. Ration their food more

slowly or, if you have other dogs, allow them to eat in separate areas. Canines who eat in groups tend to bolt their food so others can't steal it.

■ Stop providing fatty, hard-to-digest table scraps and snacks.

■ Try elevated dog dishes, like those used for large breeds, to help prevent gas buildup.

Managing the Dog's Weight

Compare the weight of your dog with the weight of other dogs in its breed (see pages 26–38). If your dog is a mixed breed (or not described in this book), examine your model to see if it has a "waist"—a visible indention behind the ribs. Overweight dogs lack this. Next, try to feel its ribs. If you can't, the dog is overweight. (If its ribs seem too pronounced, your dog may be underweight. Consider increasing its caloric intake.)

Weighing a Dog

[1] Weigh yourself on a bathroom scale (Fig. A).

[2] Pick up the dog and weigh again (Fig. B). If the dog is particularly large, be sure to exercise caution (Fig. C).

[3] Subtract the first weight from the second weight (Fig. D).

If your dog is too large to handle in this way, ask your veterinarian if you can periodically use the clinic's scale.

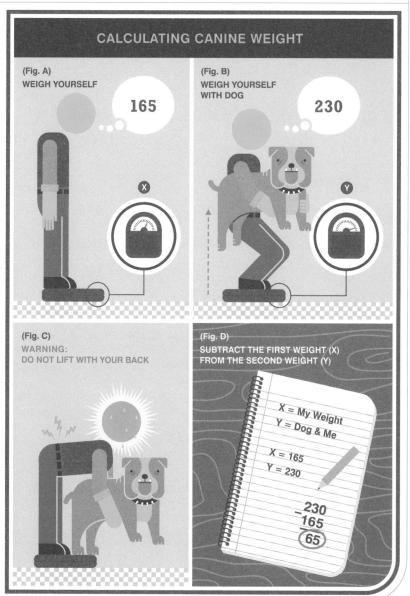

Weight Reduction

Before changing your dog's diet, develop a plan of action with your veterinarian. Weight loss in canines is a slow process with several health risks. In some cases a special diet may be needed, or there may be other complicating concerns to consider, such as diabetes. Weight loss can be accomplished either by giving the dog less of its current food or switching it to a low-calorie "diet" product.

Keep the following tips in mind as you proceed with your program:

■ Weight loss should in most cases not exceed 8 ounces to 1 pound (225–450 g) per week.

■ During this time the dog should (if your vet concurs) also receive extra exercise.

■ Avoid fatty treats. Reward the canine with praise, or offer low-calorie tidbits such as broccoli, green beans, or carrots.

■ If the dog seems unsatisfied with the amount of food it receives, try serving it several, smaller meals a day.

■ If you have multiple canines, feed them in separate locations so the dieting dog does not receive extra food.

■ Be sure the dog has plenty of water at all times.

■ Be sure all family members understand the diet plan. One person providing unauthorized food can disrupt the program.

■ Weigh the dog weekly and keep track of its progress.

■ Remember: A dog loses roughly 1 pound (.5 kg) of weight for every 3,500 calories it expends.

Average Daily Water Intake Requirement*

BODY WEIGHT	WATER
■ 5 pounds/2 kg	■ 7 ounces/207 ml
■ 10 pounds/4.5 kg	■ 14 ounces/414 ml
■ 20 pounds/9 kg	■ 24 ounces/710 ml
■ 30 pounds/13.5 kg	■ 33 ounces/975 ml
■ 40 pounds/18 kg	■ 41 ounces/1.2 l
■ 50 pounds/22.5 kg	■ 48 ounces/1.4 l
■ 60 pounds/27 kg	■ 55 ounces/1.6 l
■ 70 pounds/31.5 kg	■ 62 ounces/1.8 l
■ 80 pounds/36 kg	■ 69 ounces/2 l
■ 90 pounds/41 kg	■ 75 ounces/2.2 l
■ 100 pounds/45.5 kg	■ 82 ounces/2.4 l

*Requirements include water absorbed from food and snacks.

MODEL K-9.06 *Shih Tzu*

SHAM POOCH

[Chapter 6]

Exterior Maintenance

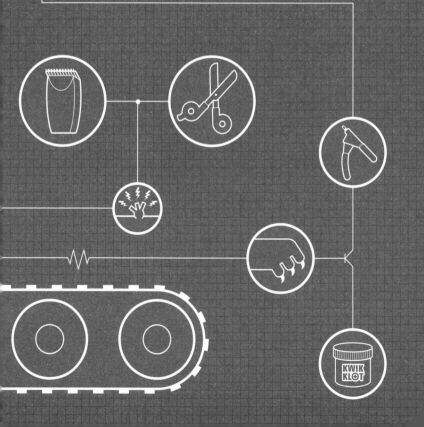

The amount of exterior detailing dogs require varies greatly from model to model. For instance, while the coats of shorthaired varieties are relatively easy to maintain, those with longer coats (collies, Old English sheepdogs) will almost certainly require regular professional attention. However, many issues are the same regardless of the breed, including nail upkeep and bathing protocols. Whatever your model, regular exterior maintenance will ensure that your canine functions in top operating condition.

Understanding the Coat

Most dog models include three kinds of hair—tactile hair, an outercoat, and an undercoat. The undercoat, also called the secondary coat, is made of dense, soft fur. It provides both insulation and support for the outercoat. The outercoat is composed of long, stiff guard hairs that protect the undercoat. The last type, tactile hair, includes the whiskers and other stiff facial hairs that provide sensory information about the outside world.

The heaviest shedders are dogs with well-developed double coats—a layer of long, coarse hair over short, dense hair. Double-coated dogs (including the Akita, Pomeranian, Newfoundland, and Siberian husky) will generally lose their undercoats twice each year and their outercoats annually. The onset of shedding is linked to hormonal changes triggered by changes in the length of the day. A dog may also "drop its coat" (shed extensively) after a physically traumatic situation such as surgery or giving birth.

Dogs that lack double coats, or that live inside, may shed all year long instead of seasonally. Other models, including poodles and many terriers, do not shed at all.

Overview of Dog Hair Varieties

**Your model will come with any of the following exterior finishes prein-
stalled.**

Long Hair: Found on such models as Old English sheepdogs, Newfoundlands, collies, golden retrievers, etc. Longhaired coats need daily brushing
to prevent tangles and excessive shedding.

Short Hair: Found on such models as beagles and pointers. This type of
coat calls for much less maintenance than other varieties, but it still requires
combing and/or brushing on a regular basis.

Nonshedding Hair: As the name suggests, this hair is maintained by the
unit year-round. However, it may still require regular clipping. This type of
finish can be found on poodles and bichons frises.

Long and Silky Hair: Found on such models as Yorkshire terriers, Pekingese,
and Afghan hounds. Without regular maintenance, these coats will quickly
become matted.

Smooth Hair: These coats can be easily groomed with a brush. Smooth
hair can be found on such breeds as Dobermans, greyhounds, and Labrador retrievers.

Wiry: Found on most terrier breeds, as well as schnauzers. Wirehaired
dogs need regular combing and clipping to prevent matting. They can also
be "hand stripped" (whereby loose hair is plucked from the coat), but this
process can take hours, even for a small dog.

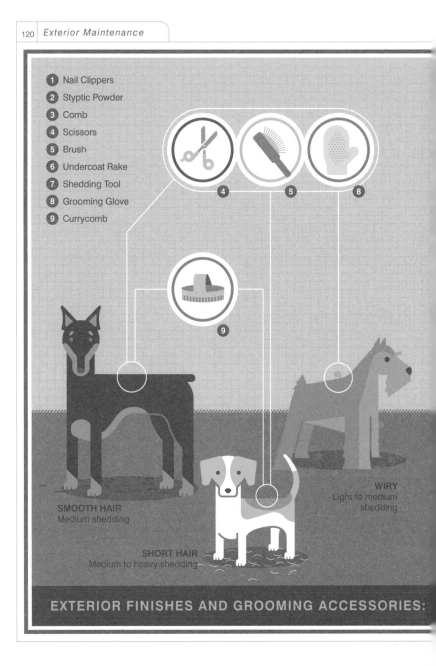

1 Nail Clippers
2 Styptic Powder
3 Comb
4 Scissors
5 Brush
6 Undercoat Rake
7 Shedding Tool
8 Grooming Glove
9 Currycomb

SMOOTH HAIR
Medium shedding

SHORT HAIR
Medium to heavy shedding

WIRY
Light to medium shedding

EXTERIOR FINISHES AND GROOMING ACCESSORIES:

ALL MODELS REQUIRE:

NONSHEDDING HAIR

LONG & SILKY HAIR
Heavy shedding

LONG HAIR
Heavy shedding

HAIRLESS

Most models should be groomed on a daily basis.

Hairless: These models include such oddities as the Chinese Crested, but there are no true "hairless" breeds. All mammals have at least some hair. For these breeds skin care (particularly sunburn protection) is extremely important.

General Coat Maintenance

To minimize deposits of hair in the house, groom your dog regularly. It is advisable, if possible, to begin brushing a puppy at an early age. It will become used to, and may even enjoy, the process. Almost all dogs should be brushed thoroughly every day to remove dirt and loose hair, to prevent tangles and matting, and to disperse natural oils throughout the coat.

EXPERT TIP: Grooming is an excellent time to examine your dog for irritated skin, lumps, bumps, ticks, fleas, and any other problem that might require veterinary attention.

Grooming Tools

The following accessories will aid in the maintenance of the dog's exterior finish.

Brush: It is important to select a brush that is suitable for your dog's coat. The ideal tool is a soft wire brush that can remove tangles without irritating skin.

Comb: Usually made of steel and featuring both fine and coarse teeth, this tool can remove burrs and tangles and bring order to the coat of a longhaired dog.

Currycomb: Often made of rubber, this tool removes loose hair from short-haired breeds while also massaging the skin.

Grooming Glove: Covered with nubby, hair-catching material, the glove is useful for face grooming, and for brushing dogs with extremely short hair.

Nail Clippers: There are two basic types—guillotine-style clippers and standard scissors-style clippers. Both work well.

Scissors: Excellent for removing particularly stubborn tangles or burrs.

Shedding Tool: This bladelike device with serrated edges is ideal for removing excess fur from longhaired breeds.

Styptic Powder: This blood-clotting powder (available at most retailers) will quickly stop bleeding caused by trimming a dog's nails too closely.

Undercoat Rake: As the name implies, this tool removes loose hair from the dense undercoat of longhaired and thick-haired breeds, such as the husky and Irish setter.

Selecting a Professional Groomer

While owners can handle the day-to-day maintenance tasks described in this chapter, more extensive work should be left to experts. Most veterinarians keep lists of recommended groomers; a few even employ groomers on staff. Additional sources for recommendations include friends, reputable purebred breeders, and boarding kennels.

If your model has special needs (for instance, if it is geriatric or requires a medicinal shampoo regimen), make sure your choice is equipped to meet them. Also, be sure the groomer does not tranquilize dogs before handling them. Make a point of visiting the salon during business hours for a surprise inspection. Are the facilities clean? Are the dogs well-treated? What you pay will vary based on the breed, the amount of hair involved, and its condition. Depending on the model, grooming may be necessary once or twice a year, or as often as every 6 weeks.

⚠ *CAUTION: Before taking your dog to a groomer, make sure its vaccinations (especially for* bordetella*, or kennel cough) are current.*

Removing Mats

Mats are amalgams of tightly tangled hair usually pressed close to the dog's skin. When ignored, they can cause severe discomfort and skin irritation. Upon discovering a mat, use fingers and a comb to untangle as much as possible. If the mat, or a portion thereof, cannot be untangled, carefully cut it out by first placing a comb between the hair and the dog's skin, then trim out the clump with scissors. Since the mat is usually very close to the skin, the comb will act as a guard against cuts.

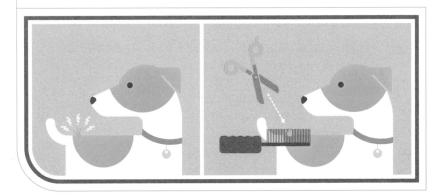

Bathing

To ensure a quality finish on the dog's exterior coating, you should bathe the animal on a regular basis. This experience can be an enjoyable one, especially if the dog is introduced to the process during puppyhood. For most breeds, a bath every few months should suffice, unless the animal tends to dirty itself more often. Brush the dog before bathing it to remove mats and tangles.

⚠️ *CAUTION: Bathing the dog too frequently may lead to dry skin and/or skin irritation; if you must wash the dog often, or own a breed predisposed to dry skin, use a canine-formulated conditioning shampoo.*

[1] Place a rubber mat in the bathtub (Fig. A). This will give the dog a secure footing and will help it relax.

[2] Be sure all supplies are within your reach (Fig. B).

[3] Put a cotton ball in each of the dog's ears to keep out water (Fig. C).

[4] Place the dog in the tub. If the canine is a large model and you are unsure of your ability to lift it, seek help.

[5] Rinse the dog thoroughly with warm water, using a spray hose if available. Hold the nozzle as close to the dog's body as possible. Do not spray it in the face.

⚠️ *EXPERT TIP: Throughout this process, it is important to stroke and reassure the dog frequently (especially if it is not used to bathing).*

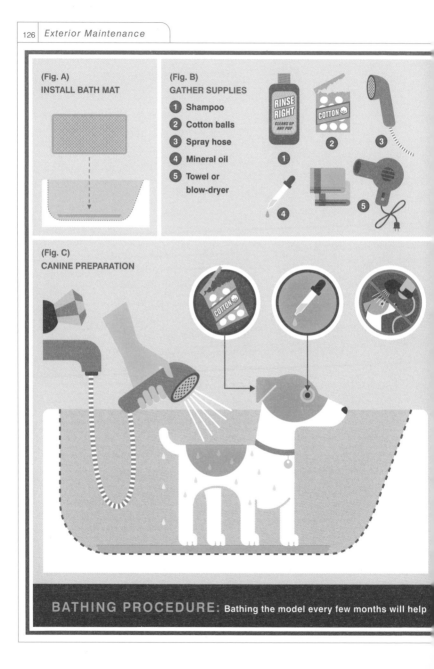

(Fig. A)
INSTALL BATH MAT

(Fig. B)
GATHER SUPPLIES
1 Shampoo
2 Cotton balls
3 Spray hose
4 Mineral oil
5 Towel or blow-dryer

(Fig. C)
CANINE PREPARATION

BATHING PROCEDURE: Bathing the model every few months will help

127

(Fig. D)
APPLY DOG-FORMULATED SHAMPOO

(Fig. E)
DON'T FORGET TO WASH

1 Waste port
2 Toes
3 Behind the ears
4 Under the chin

(Fig. F)
CHOOSE DRYING METHOD

OR

LOW

to maintain a quality exterior finish. But washing it too often will dry the skin.

[6] Apply a dog-formulated shampoo, in small amounts, working from tail to head (Fig. D).

[7] Be sure the waste port, toes, and the areas behind the ears and under the chin are clean (Fig. E).

⚠ *CAUTION: Avoid getting shampoo in the dog's eyes. A drop of mineral oil in the corner of each eye immediately prior to bath time prevents irritation.*

[8] Rinse the dog thoroughly with warm water. Begin at the head. Squeeze excess water from the coat. Remove the cotton balls from its ears.

[9] Dry the dog with a towel or hair dryer (Fig. F). Dogs with kinky or long coats, including the Maltese, bichon frise, and poodle, look better blow-dried. Keep the dryer on its lowest setting, and never direct the air flow into the dog's face.

⚠ *CAUTION: Some breeds (including basset hounds and many members of the spaniel family) have excessively oily coats. If not bathed and properly groomed, the oil can become rancid and cause a dandruff-like condition called primary seborrhea. Medicinal shampoos can correct the problem. Consult your veterinarian for details.*

Ears

The ears should be checked weekly for signs of unpleasant odor, redness, and/or inflammation, all of which should be examined by a veterinarian. To remove excess dirt, use a baby oil- or alcohol-soaked cotton ball. Do not probe too deeply into the ear canal. Proper ear

maintenance is particularly important in "droopy-eared" breeds (basset hounds, beagles, bloodhounds, etc.), because air may not circulate freely to their ear canals.

Eyes

A healthy dog's eyes should always be shiny and wide open. During grooming, gently wipe away any discharge that has accumulated around them (a warm washcloth may help). Consult your veterinarian if the discharge is green or yellow. White-haired dogs may develop discoloration in the fur around their eyes from excessive tearing. These stains can sometimes be reduced by applying commercial solutions available at all pet stores. Do not attempt this without consulting your veterinarian.

Teeth

A dog's teeth are subject to such problems as plaque buildup, periodontal disease, and occasional cavities. The teeth should be cleaned at least twice per week with a pet toothpaste and a toothbrush with soft bristles. Regular professional cleaning by a veterinarian is also a must.

⚠ *EXPERT TIP: Never use human toothpaste, which can upset dogs' stomachs.*

Anal Glands

Extremely unpleasant odors can result if the dog's anal sacs (two small glands bracketing the anus) become full and/or infected. If the dog frequently licks its rectal area, or if the dog frequently drags this area across the floor, be sure to mention this behavior to a veterinarian. Usually, the best way to address this problem is to regularly empty or "express" the anal glands. This procedure can be done by a professional groomer or at a veterinarian's office. With proper vet-guided instruction, dog owners can learn to execute the procedure themselves.

Nails

Nails should be trimmed approximately twice per month. Use a purpose-designed clipper (see page 123) and be sure to have cotton swabs and a bottle of styptic powder nearby. This commercially available blood-clotting powder can be used to stop bleeding if you accidentally trim a nail too closely.

[1] Instruct the dog to sit beside you and take one of its paws in your hand. A smaller dog can sit on your lap. Alternatively, have the dog roll onto its stomach on the floor.

[2] Clip the first nail in stages. Be careful not to trim the quick (the part of the nail containing nerves and blood vessels). If you cannot locate the quick, stop cutting at the spot where the nail begins to curve downward.

EXPERT TIP: *If you have trouble spotting the quick, try trimming nails just after a bath, when it will be more visible. Applying baby oil to nails can also make the quick easier to see.*

[3] If you accidentally clip the quick, comfort the dog and apply styptic powder to the nail using a moist cotton swab. Press firmly against the nail for 10 seconds.

TRIMMING THE NAILS

1. Trim nail at angle shown
2. Do not cut the quick (dark area)

If you cut the quick:
3. Dip cotton swab in water
4. Dip cotton swab in styptic powder and apply to the bleeding quick

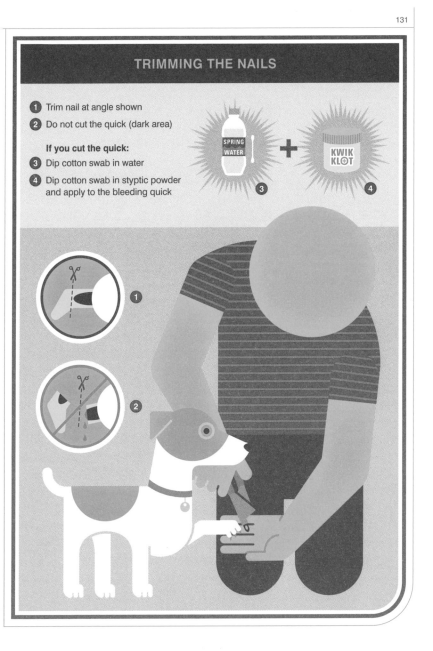

[4] Repeat the clipping process until all nails are trimmed. Each nail should be cut at a 45-degree angle away from the dog so the nail is flush with the floor when the dog is on its feet.

[5] Remember to trim the dewclaws, located on the inside of each leg.

Emergency Cleanups

Whenever you locate foreign or unidentified substances on your dog's coat, it is best to remove them immediately. Otherwise, the dog may ingest them via licking, which may lead to malfunction.

Burrs: Most can be removed with careful use of a metal comb. Deeply entangled burrs can often be released by working vegetable oil into the affected area. If this method fails to work, carefully remove the burrs with scissors.

Chewing Gum: Apply ice to the gum to reduce its stickiness, then clip from fur. Alternatively, there are several commercial products that facilitate gum removal without haircutting.

Paint: If it is a water-based paint, soak the affected area in water for 5 minutes or longer until it becomes pliant. Then rub the affected fur between your fingers to remove it. Any other type of paint will require careful clipping and trimming.

⚠ *CAUTION: Never use paint thinner, turpentine, gasoline, or any other such solvents on your dog.*

Skunk: If your dog is sprayed by a skunk, you can de-scent the model with a thorough bath in tomato juice. Place the dog in a basin filled with tomato juice; allow the exterior coat to soak in the juice for several minutes, then rinse and repeat. The dog may require several baths (over several days) before the scent disappears.

Tar: In many cases the tar-coated hair will have to be clipped away. However, petroleum jelly can sometimes remove the substance. Rub some into a small portion of the affected area, then wipe away the broken-up tar with a clean cloth. Repeat as many times as necessary. Bathe the dog with a degreasing shampoo afterward.

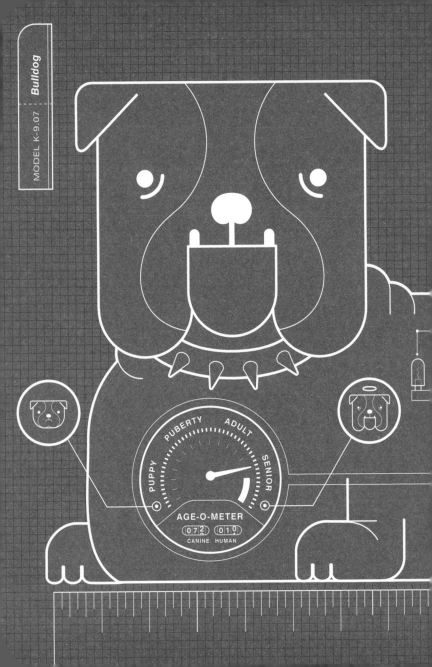

Growth and Development

Puppy Growth Stages

Unlike most consumer products, which can only be upgraded by purchasing and installing expensive peripherals, the dog has the ability to increase its cognitive and mechanical capacities on its own. This phenomenon is most obvious in puppies, who in a matter of months upgrade from fragile, highly dependent units into fully mature systems. This section offers an overview of that remarkable process.

Birth to 8 Weeks

The puppy is entirely dependent on its mother. Puppies are born with sealed eyes and ear canals. Walking begins at 16 days. Eyelids open at the age of 2 weeks, while ear canals open after approximately 17 days. Waste elimination without assistance from the mother (who licks the genital area to stimulate the process) begins at 23 days of age. At 25 days, puppies begin responding to sights and sounds. Baby teeth appear at 4 to 6 weeks; consumption of solid food begins at the same time.

Programming Milestones: Little true learning is possible at this time, though some rudimentary socialization can be accomplished. For instance, frequent, gentle handling will help the newborn become acclimated to people. Remember that the puppy must remain with its mother and littermates during this important period. Only they can help it download much of the programming necessary for proper dog behavior.

8 to 15 Weeks

Full weaning takes place at or before 8 weeks. Puppies can be supplied with small amounts of solid food (as a supplement to milk) as early as their fourth week, when their first set of teeth will begin to emerge. Choose a specially formulated puppy food that is thinned to the consistency of gruel. As the weeks pass, the amount of solid matter in the gruel should be increased.

Programming Milestones: This is the prime age for learning to interface with humans. Eight weeks is also the accepted time for a puppy to be removed from the litter and transferred to its adopted family. Crate training, leash training, and house-training instruction can begin.

16 Weeks to 11 Months

Puberty begins at 6 to 8 months of age. A female dog will reach sexual maturity between the ages of 9 and 15 months; males reach sexual maturity between 7 and 12 months. (See page 141 for more information.)

Programming Milestones: At 12 to 20 weeks, the puppy may become fearful if left alone or in new places. A puppy socialization class can mitigate the problem, which usually passes with time. Basic obedience-training downloads are best accomplished at this time.

12 Months

By the age of 1 year, puppies will have made the transformation into adult dogs. In most cases, you will want to switch the dog's fuel supply from a puppy-formulated mixture to a blend more suitable for adults.

Programming Milestones: The dog will ideally be fully socialized to humans at this point, and you may also notice an increased attention span. This is an excellent time to initiate advanced obedience training.

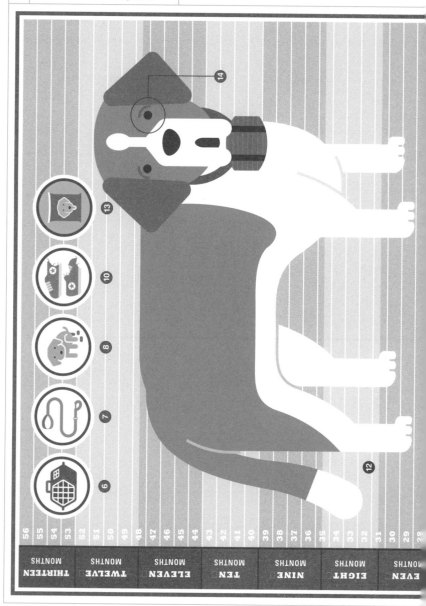

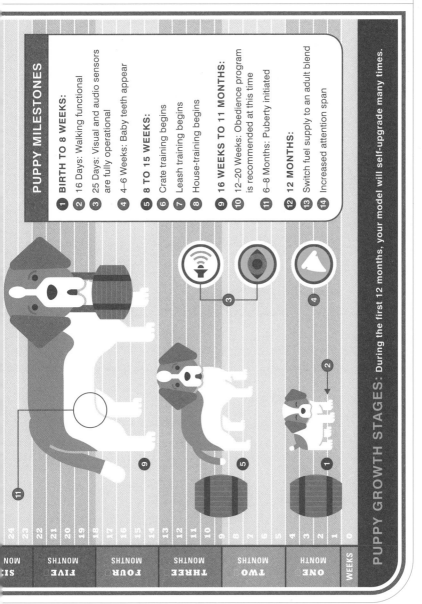

PUPPY MILESTONES

① BIRTH TO 8 WEEKS:
- ② 16 Days: Walking functional
- ③ 25 Days: Visual and audio sensors are fully operational
- ④ 4–6 Weeks: Baby teeth appear

⑤ 8 TO 15 WEEKS:
- ⑥ Crate training begins
- ⑦ Leash training begins
- ⑧ House-training begins

⑨ 16 WEEKS TO 11 MONTHS:
- ⑩ 12–20 Weeks: Obedience program is recommended at this time
- ⑪ 6–8 Months: Puberty initiated

⑫ 12 MONTHS:
- ⑬ Switch fuel supply to an adult blend
- ⑭ Increased attention span

PUPPY GROWTH STAGES: During the first 12 months, your model will self-upgrade many times.

WEEKS	ONE MONTH	TWO MONTHS	THREE MONTHS	FOUR MONTHS	FIVE MONTHS	SIX MON...

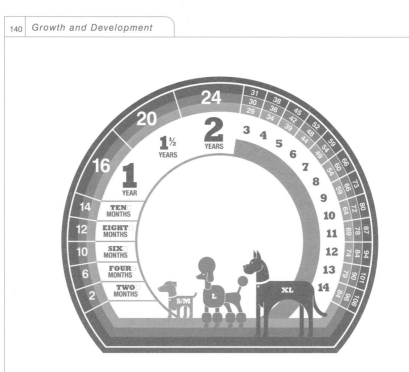

Calculating Age in "Dog Years"

A popular misconception is that dogs age 7 years for each calendar year. In fact, canine aging is much more rapid during the first 2 years of a dog's life.

After the first 2 years the ratio settles down to 5 to 1 for small and medium breeds. For large breeds the rate is 6 to 1, and for giant breeds the rate is 7 to 1. Thus, at 10 years of age a Great Dane would be 80 years old while a pug would only be 64.

Teeth Development

The dog's first teeth will appear between 4 and 6 weeks of age, at approximately the same time the puppy is introduced to solid food. This first set is composed of baby teeth, as in humans. The front incisors

are replaced by permanent teeth at around 3 to 4 months. Permanent canines (incisors) appear during the sixth month; premolars arrive at 4 to 6 months and molars at 5 to 7 months. Once their permanent teeth come in, puppies develop an almost-overwhelming urge to chew, which helps set their teeth firmly in their jaws. To keep your canine from chewing furniture or other valuables, provide it with plenty of toys (and supervision).

Diet Requirements

Puppies should receive a high-quality diet specifically designed for their needs. Ask your veterinarian to recommend an appropriate commercial brand. In general, puppies should receive no more per feeding than they can consume in 5 to 10 minutes. Puppies 6 to 12 weeks old usually are fed three times a day; two times a day when aged 12 weeks to 6 months; and one or two times daily when older than 6 months.

⚠ *CAUTION: Puppies should never be given vitamins or dietary supplements of any kind unless recommended by a veterinarian.*

Sexual Maturity

The age of sexual maturity varies from breed to breed and from individual to individual. The range is as wide as 9 to 15 months for females and 7 to 12 months for males. Females typically go into heat (estrus) for 3-week periods twice yearly. While in estrus, the canine is receptive to the advances of males and is capable of breeding. It is important to keep the female confined or under close observation during these times, because she can attract male dogs from great distances.

Male dogs have no "cycle." They can breed year-round and will act whenever they encounter a receptive female. Male sexual maturity may also manifest itself in leg humping and in the lifting of the leg during urination. (See "Spaying and Neutering," below.)

EXPERT TIP: As with human adolescents, dogs entering puberty often experience sometimes difficult personality changes. Extra exercise, plus spaying/neutering before puberty, can help mitigate such difficulties.

Spaying and Neutering

It is the duty of every responsible pet owner to have his or her canine spayed or neutered. Unwanted litters contribute to a vast oversupply of dogs in the United States. Unless you plan to breed your dog (which is not recommended, except in the case of highly valued purebred models), it should be sterilized before reaching sexual maturity. For males this is called *neutering* (removal of the testicles); for females, *spaying* (removal of the ovaries and uterus). Neutered males are generally less aggressive, less prone to roam, and less excitable than their unaltered peers. They also suffer from fewer health problems such as prostate troubles and testicular cancer.

Likewise, females spayed before puberty have their chances of contracting mammary cancer (an extremely common malady) reduced to near zero. Also, the danger of ovarian cysts, uterine infections, and cancers of the reproductive tract (all very common malfunctions) are eliminated. Neutered and spayed dogs tend to gain weight more easily, but this can be countered by feeding 10 to 20 percent less food and increasing exercise. In most cases, neutering and spaying can be performed at any time past the age of 16 weeks.

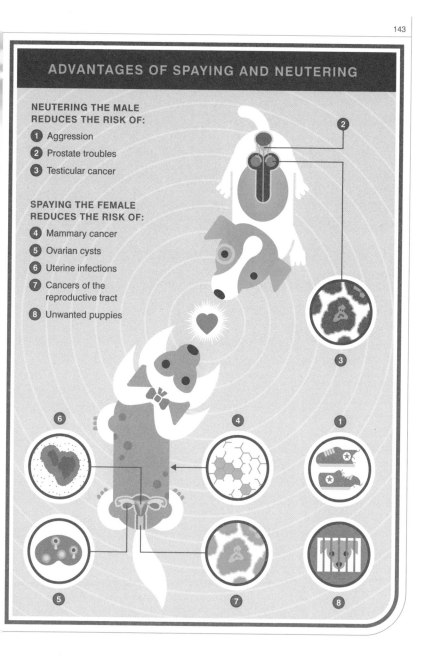

ADVANTAGES OF SPAYING AND NEUTERING

**NEUTERING THE MALE
REDUCES THE RISK OF:**

1 Aggression
2 Prostate troubles
3 Testicular cancer

**SPAYING THE FEMALE
REDUCES THE RISK OF:**

4 Mammary cancer
5 Ovarian cysts
6 Uterine infections
7 Cancers of the
   reproductive tract
8 Unwanted puppies

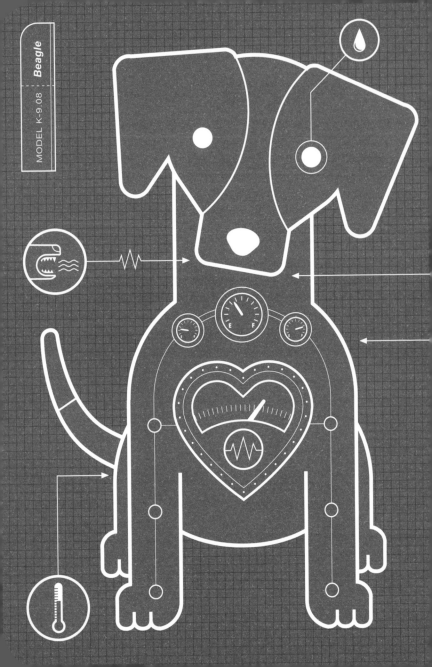

Chapter 8

Interior Maintenance

When dealing with mechanical or software glitches, dog owners can call on a vast, highly developed service and support infrastructure for assistance. This chapter explains how to locate and utilize a qualified service provider in your vicinity. It will also describe how to recognize and manage smaller problems that can be easily fixed in your own home.

Selecting a Service Provider

One of the first tasks a new dog owner must accomplish is selecting the right veterinarian. The ideal candidate will be available to service your pet for its entire lifespan. He or she can maintain long-term treatment and immunization records; chart reactions to specific medications; even develop an understanding of your dog's particular programming quirks. This extensive knowledge base is helpful during minor emergencies and can mean the difference between life and death during major ones. Here are some other guidelines to consider when selecting a service provider.

■ When considering candidates, consult friends who own dogs. Breed clubs can also provide lists of recommended doctors, including, in some cases, veterinarians with special knowledge of particular models.

■ Schedule an appointment with the veterinarians you are considering. Discuss your dog and its specific needs. Do you feel comfortable with the vet? What professional organizations does he or she belong to?

■ Examine the facility itself. Does it look and smell clean? What range of services does it provide? How are emergency after-hours calls handled?

■ Make sure your choice is a good fit logistically. Does the clinic keep business hours that are convenient for you? Is the office conveniently located? Patronizing a vet with odd hours and an out-of-the-way location is difficult at best, life-threatening at worst.

⚠ **EXPERT TIP:** *You might want to select a veterinarian before acquiring a dog. If you are unsure about which model to choose, a veterinarian can provide expert advice.*

Conducting a Home Maintenance Inspection

Dog owners should inspect their models regularly for potential health problems. The best time to do this is during the dog's regular grooming regimen. Here are some systems to review.

Mouth: Teeth should be white and gums should be pink (unless they are naturally pigmented black). There should be no lumps or bumps in the mouth. The model should not emit "doggy breath" (see page 154).

Eyes: A healthy dog should have clear eyes with no discharge, squinting, irritation, or cloudiness.

Ears: The interior of the ears should be pink, odorless, and free of dark-colored discharge. There should be no signs of tenderness, pain, or itching.

Weight: If you cannot feel the dog's ribs, the unit may be overweight. If the ribs are very pronounced, however, the canine could be underweight.

Paws: Check the feet for damage to the pads. Make sure the nails and dewclaws (if present) are trimmed and in good condition.

Waste Port: Make sure the anal area is clean, dry, and free of bumps and welts.

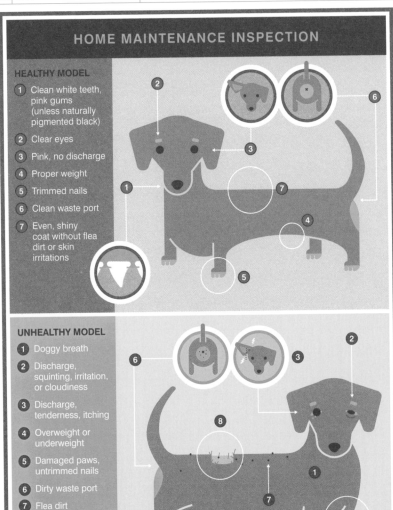

HOME MAINTENANCE INSPECTION

HEALTHY MODEL

1. Clean white teeth, pink gums (unless naturally pigmented black)
2. Clear eyes
3. Pink, no discharge
4. Proper weight
5. Trimmed nails
6. Clean waste port
7. Even, shiny coat without flea dirt or skin irritations

UNHEALTHY MODEL

1. Doggy breath
2. Discharge, squinting, irritation, or cloudiness
3. Discharge, tenderness, itching
4. Overweight or underweight
5. Damaged paws, untrimmed nails
6. Dirty waste port
7. Flea dirt
8. Bald spots
9. Excessive shedding

Skin: Use a comb to examine the skin. Look for "flea dirt" (excrement from fleas that resembles grains of pepper). Skin should be free of odor, grease, scabs, flakes, and other irritations.

Coat: Check the coat for bald spots, dullness, and/or excessive, unwarranted shedding.

Visiting Your Service Provider

Barring emergencies, most dogs will require a handful of veterinary visits during their first year of life and annual visits thereafter. Listed below is an approximate guideline of when you should expect to have the dog serviced and what you can expect a veterinarian to do.

Age 6–8 Weeks

- Physical examination
- DHPP immunization (a combination vaccination for distemper, hepatitis, parainfluenza, and parvovirus)
- Stool exam for parasites
- Deworming
- Begin heartworm preventative medication and (if seasonally appropriate) flea preventative

Age 10–12 Weeks

- Physical examination
- DHLPP immunization (DHPP plus vaccination for leptospirosis)
- Deworming

■ Kennel cough (Bordetella) vaccination

■ Administer heartworm preventative medication and (if seasonally appropriate) flea preventative

Age 14–16 Weeks

■ Physical examination

■ DHLPP immunization

■ Kennel cough (Bordetella) vaccination

■ Rabies vaccination

■ Administer heartworm preventative medication and (if seasonally appropriate) flea preventative

Annually

■ Physical examination

■ DHLPP booster immunization

■ Kennel cough (Bordetella) booster

■ Rabies booster (if state regulations mandate)

■ Deworming (if necessary)

■ Heartworm blood test

■ Wellness testing in mature dogs (initiated at 5 to 7 years to evaluate kidneys, liver, blood sugar, and other organ functions)

⚠ *CAUTION: In certain regions of the world, additional vaccinations, such as for Lyme disease, may be recommended or required. Currently, there is much debate about which immunizations to administer and how often they should be given. Consult your veterinarian for recommendations and the latest data.*

Potentially Major Hardware Glitches

Throughout its life, the average dog will display numerous mechanical "hiccups," most of which it will quickly resolve on its own. If the symptom(s) persist or worsen over a 24-hour period, however, you should consider seeking professional assistance.

Bleeding: A superficial cut or scrape can be treated at home. Deeper injuries or puncture wounds require immediate veterinary attention—as does persistent, uncontrolled bleeding from a wound or orifice. Occasional, slight bleeding during bowel movements is usually not a serious problem.

Breathing Difficulty: Prolonged respiratory distress (coughing, sneezing, labored breath, and so on) may signal anything from choking to heart failure. Consult your veterinarian immediately.

Collapse: If your dog has fallen and cannot stand up, contact your veterinarian immediately and prepare to take the dog to the clinic. Try to remember what transpired in the moments before the attack; knowledge of these events may be helpful in determining a cause.

Diarrhea: A brief bout can be triggered by something as minor as a change in diet. If the problem persists for 24 hours, consult your veterinarian. Prolonged bouts can lead to dehydration. The skin of dehydrated dogs loses its elasticity and will not immediately snap back when gently pulled.

Ear Discharge: If the normal, waxy discharge becomes excessive, takes on a new color, or develops a bad odor, consult your veterinarian.

Excessive Water Consumption: This can be an indicator, particularly in an older or overweight dog, of diabetes or kidney malfunction.

Eye Discharge: A certain amount of discharge from the eyes is normal. Excessive or green and/or yellow discharge should be reported to your veterinarian. Red and/or swollen eyes should also be checked.

Fever: A dog's normal core temperature is between 100.5 and 102.5°F (38–39°C). Any body temperature higher than 103°F (39.5°C) is considered a fever. Temperatures higher than 104.5°F (40.25°C) necessitate an immediate trip to the veterinarian. (See "Measuring the Dog's Core Temperature," page 159.)

Gum Discoloration: Pink gums indicate normal oxygenation of the gum tissue. Pale, white, blue, or yellow gums require veterinary attention. To assess your dog's circulation, briefly press on the gums and release. If it takes less than 1 second—or more than 3 seconds—for the area to return to its normal pink color, some sort of vascular disorder may be responsible.

Inappropriate Urination: In a house-trained adult dog, regular, unauthorized urination may signal problems such as kidney disorders, diabetes, a urinary tract infection, or even the onset of senility.

Limping (Persistent): Could indicate anything from a sprain to the onset of hip dysplasia or osteoarthritis. If the problem persists for more than an hour or two, consult a veterinarian.

Loss of Appetite: Can denote anything from the onset of an infectious disease to severe pain to a psychological imbalance. However, all dogs "go off their feed" occasionally, so there is no need to worry unless the problem persists for more than 24 hours.

Seizures: Could signal any number of malfunctions, from epilepsy to a severe head injury. Remain with the pet during the episode and, if possible, time how long it lasts. Once it passes, consult your veterinarian. If the seizure continues for longer than 5 minutes, transport the dog (if necessary, while still seizing) to the veterinary office. Keep hands clear of the dog's mouth.

Skin Irritation: A small patch of dry skin or a small hot spot (see page 154) can be dealt with at home. Any disruption that appears red and irritated, that is seeping, or that causes the canine obvious discomfort should be professionally assessed.

Tremors: Can indicate anything from neurological damage to poisoning. Consult your veterinarian immediately.

Vomiting: A dog who vomits once or twice in a 24-hour period should be monitored. In many cases, the problem will simply go away. However, persistent vomiting for 12 hours necessitates a trip to the vet. Vomiting blood necessitates immediate veterinary attention.

Weight Loss: Pronounced weight loss can indicate any number of disorders, including cancer. However, it could also simply mean that the dog isn't receiving enough calories. Consult your veterinarian.

Minor Hardware Glitches

Minor malfunctions can often be resolved using basic first-aid techniques. To gauge if the problem is indeed minor, ask what you would do if the same injury was sustained by a child. If you would take the child to a hospital, then take the dog to a veterinarian.

Damaged Dewclaws: Excessive nail growth, coupled with the dewclaws' lack of bony support, make them prone to lacerations if caught on carpeting, underbrush, or tall grass. If the tear is small, treat as a superficial cut (see next page). If severe, consult your veterinarian. Professional (surgical) removal of the dewclaw is often the best course of action.

Doggy Breath: May indicate gum disease, severe plaque buildup, or a number of other dental disorders. Sweet, fruity breath can indicate diabetes.

Hot Spots: These are localized allergic reactions that trigger severe itching and self-inflicted irritation (usually via licking). These moist skin lesions will cause a dog great discomfort and, if untreated, can worsen rapidly. If the area is small, clip away hair and clean with hydrogen peroxide. Clean the area daily with antibacterial and astringent products until it is completely healed. Antibiotics or hydrocortisone cream may be required. Consult your veterinarian about particularly large hot spots.

Minor Allergic Reaction: This often results from insect bites. Apply hydrocortisone cream two to three times daily.

Skin Irritation: Cleanse area, remove the causative agent, and apply hydrocortisone cream two to three times daily.

Superficial Cuts and Scrapes: Cleanse the area with mild soap and water. Baby wipes work well. Apply triple antibiotic ointment twice daily.

Torn and/or Bleeding Nail(s): If the torn portion is small and near the end of the nail, carefully remove it with a human nail trimmer (a tool ideal for trimming away small, jagged pieces). In all other instances, use a trimmer designed especially for canines. If the tear is close to the base of the nail, consult a veterinarian.

Creating a Home Repair Kit

While most medical issues should be taken to a veterinarian, some minor problems can be handled at home using the following equipment. Place all these items in one container (a small, plastic toolbox is ideal) and position it someplace easily accessible. Include the name and phone number of your veterinarian, along with the phone number of the nearest animal emergency clinic.

- Roll cotton and cotton balls
- Gauze pads and gauze tape
- Scissors
- Eyewash
- Oral syringes
- Large towel
- Exam gloves
- 1-inch surgical tape
- Ice pack
- Thermometer (preferably digital)
- Pill gun (see page 157)

You may also wish to keep a canine medical file near your home repair kit. This folder should contain all relevant information regarding your dog's medical history, including:

- Information on all immunizations the dog has received (with dates)
- A list of previously taken medications
- Current medications, including heartworm and flea preventatives
- Blood test dates and results
- Owner copies of veterinary office invoices and examination sheets, if possible (these provide a useful "paper trail" of past conditions and treatments)

Medicinal Compounds

While most human medications can be ineffective or actually harmful for dogs, several can perform useful—perhaps lifesaving—service. However, you should never administer human medications, even the ones listed below, without first consulting your veterinarian. Even useful drugs may require an adjusted dosage.

Benadryl: An antihistamine useful for insect stings/bites, vaccination reaction, itchiness, etc. Ask your veterinarian about the proper dose.

Gas-X: Just as with humans, these pills stop gas pain and bloating in canines. Other popular brands will also accomplish this. Check with your veterinarian for the right dosage.

Hydrocortisone Ointment: For treating hot spots and allergic skin reactions.

Hydrogen Peroxide: A good general disinfectant.

Isopropyl Alcohol: An even mix of isopropyl (rubbing) alcohol and vinegar is useful for cleaning ears.

Pedialyte: Rehydrates and replaces electrolytes in dogs suffering from diarrhea.

Triple Antibiotic Ointment: For treating superficial cuts and abrasions.

Administering Pills

If you will be administering pills on a regular basis, you may wish to invest in a pill gun. This device consists of a long plastic tube with a plunger at one end, and is designed to "shoot" a pill directly into the dog's mouth port. If you do not have a pill gun, employ the following procedure instead.

[1] Using your nondominant hand, grasp the dog's head (Fig. A). Place your hand on top of muzzle, with thumb on one side and fingers on the other.

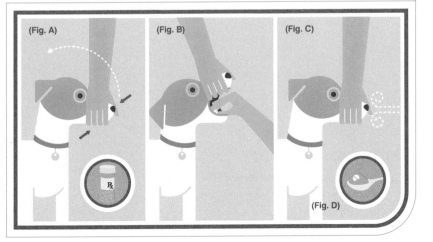

(Fig. A)　　　(Fig. B)　　　(Fig. C)

(Fig. D)

[2] Raise the dog's nose upward. Squeeze firmly behind the canine or "eye" teeth until the mouth opens (Fig. B).

[3] Place the pill between the thumb and forefinger of your dominant hand, then use the remaining three fingers of the same hand to open the lower jaw farther.

[4] Place the pill far back in the dog's mouth, close the mouth, and keep it closed (Fig. C).

EXPERT TIP: *Briefly blowing on its nose will stimulate the canine to swallow. Also, many dogs will take pills hidden in peanut butter or some other treat (Fig. D).*

[5] Offer a treat after the pill session, to make future encounters easier.

Measuring the Dog's Heart Rate

A normal, alert dog's pulse can range from 60 to 140 beats per minute. If it falls outside this range, contact your veterinarian immediately.

[1] Encourage the dog to lie down, then roll it onto its right side.

[2] Bend the front left leg, drawing the elbow back until it touches the chest.

[3] Place either your hand or a stethoscope over this spot.

[4] Count heartbeats while looking at the second hand of your watch. Count for 60 seconds. Alternately, count for 6 seconds and add a zero.

Measuring the Dog's Core Temperature

Use only a digital thermometer. Be aware that ear thermometers are incompatible with the structure of the canine ear canal.

[**1**] Have an assistant hold the head and front of the dog (Fig. E).

[**2**] Lubricate the thermometer with petroleum jelly or some other commercial lubricant (Fig. F).

[**3**] Lift the tail and insert the thermometer into the rectum (Fig. G) about 1 inch (2.5 cm). Hold it in place until the thermometer beeps.

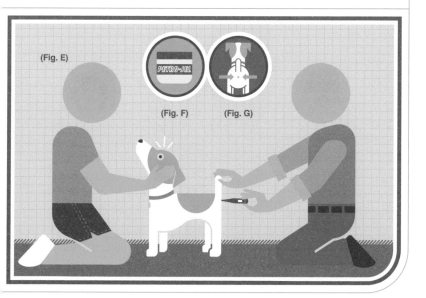

(Fig. E)

PETRO-JEL

(Fig. F)

(Fig. G)

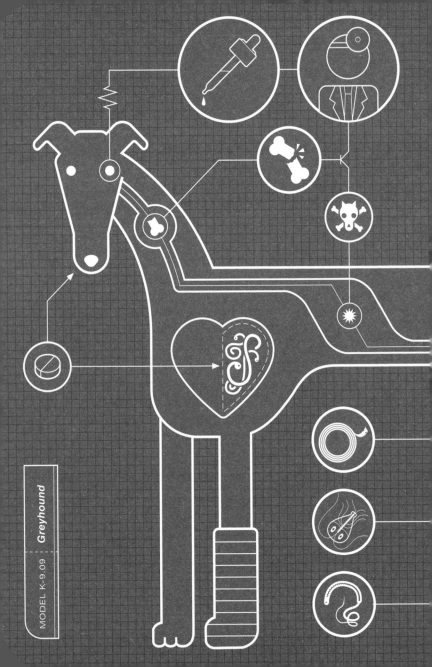

MODEL K-9.09 *Greyhound*

[Chapter 9]

Emergency
Maintenance

The following section offers a brief look at the most prominent—and dangerous—of canine-related malfunctions. Though the list is daunting, remember that proper maintenance and expert intervention can correct or mitigate most of these difficulties. For quick reference, disorders are flagged with a cross (✚) to indicate that immediate veterinary attention is required. A skull (☠) designates potentially lethal disorders.

Contagious Diseases

Vaccines are available for all of these disorders and should be administered on whatever schedule your veterinarian recommends.

✚ ☠ Rabies: A viral infection usually transmitted by the bite of an infected animal, rabies causes severe, fatal nervous system damage. State laws vary, but in some locales unvaccinated pets who encounter rabid animals are euthanized immediately.

✚ ☠ Canine Distemper: This virus is the most dangerous threat to the world's canine population. Among young dogs and puppies (the most susceptible population), the death rate for infected animals can reach 80 percent. Even dogs who survive often sustain severe, irreversible neurological damage. The disease is highly contagious.

✚ Canine Parainfluenza: This virus causes a mild respiratory tract infection not unlike the flu (hence the name).

✚ ☠ Canine Leptospirosis: A bacterial disease that can cause renal damage and even kidney failure. Exposure risk varies greatly, depending on location. Your veterinarian can provide an assessment of the risk your dog faces.

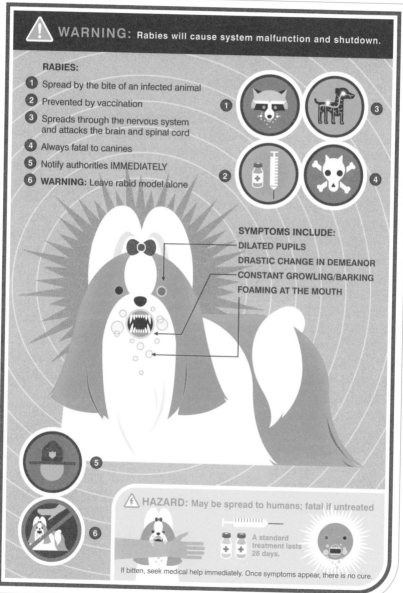

✚ ☠ Canine Parvovirus (Parvo): A very contagious viral disease that surfaced in the late 1970s, parvo attacks the intestines, white blood cells, and heart. Dogs afflicted with parvo develop severe vomiting, followed by bloody diarrhea. Intensive medical treatment for 7 to 10 days can cure many adult canines, but in puppies the disorder is often fatal.

✚ Canine Bordetella: Also known as kennel cough, this bacterial infection causes severe, chronic cough that lasts 2 to 3 weeks.

✚ Canine Coronavirus: A virus that attacks the intestinal wall, causing gastroenteritis.

✚ Lyme Disease: A tick-borne disorder that can cause neuromuscular and joint disease, along with other problems. Lyme disease can also be contracted by humans and is most common in the Northeast and Upper Midwest regions of the United States.

Chronic Diseases

✚ ☠ Cancer: Dog and human cancer rates are roughly the same; approximately half the deaths of canines over the age of 10 are a consequence of this disease. Common forms of cancer in dogs include mammary, skin, mouth, neck, lymphomid, bone, and testicular. As with human cases, canine cancer is battled using surgery, drugs, and radiation, among other methods. Success rates depend on the form of cancer, aggressiveness of treatment, and how early the problem is discovered.

✚ Heart Disease: This can be either a genetic or an acquired malfunction. Approximately 3.2 million of the dogs examined in the United States each year have some form of acquired heart disease. Most commonly, the heart valves no longer close properly, interfering with blood flow; or the walls of the heart grow thin and weak. Either condition, if left untreated, can lead to heart failure. Symptoms include coughing, lethargy, heart enlargement, and difficulty breathing. Though there is no cure for heart disease, treatment can mitigate the symptoms and provide a longer, more comfortable life.

✚ ☠ Kidney Disease: The acute form of this disorder can attack suddenly and may be triggered by anything from a minor infection to physical trauma. Severe damage to, and loss of function in, the kidneys usually results. Though treatment options exist, a canine who survives the disorder will often have severely degraded renal function. Chronic kidney disease, usually seen in older dogs, advances much more gradually. Dietary changes can often slow its course. However, the disease is progressive, with many canines eventually succumbing to kidney failure.

✚ Bladder Problems: Canines can suffer from a variety of bladder-related difficulties, most of them familiar to humans, including kidney stones, cystitis (bladder infection), and bladder cancer.

✚ Osteoarthritis: This age-related malfunction is triggered when the cushion of cartilage between bones breaks down, causing inflammation. Pain medications, dietary supplements, and lifestyle changes can mitigate its effects to a degree. If a dog is overweight, a diet and mild exercise may result in significant improvement.

Hereditary Diseases

In many cases, specific dog breeds often suffer from genetic maladies. This doesn't mean you shouldn't acquire a particular model—only that you should be alert to its special needs. The following is a partial listing of possible maladies and some of the breeds they affect.

Back Problems: Often seen in beagles, cocker spaniels, dachshunds, and Pekingese.

Deafness: Sometimes seen in bull terriers (interestingly, only in the all-white models) and Dalmatians.

Diabetes: A fairly common problem for dachshunds.

Epilepsy: Sometimes seen in beagles, cocker spaniels, Labrador retrievers, and German shepherds.

Eye Problems: Difficulties can range from a predisposition to cataracts to corneal ulceration to extra eyelashes. Breeds prone to genetic eye conditions include (but are not confined to) Border collies, boxers, Chow Chows, cocker spaniels, Dobermans, Pekingese, poodles, Rottweilers, and schnauzers.

Heart Defects/Problems: Commonly seen in boxers, cavalier King Charles spaniels, and bulldogs. Difficulties can range from malformed heart valves to premature deterioration of the heart muscle.

Hip Dysplasia: A hip condition triggering sometimes severe lameness in the hindquarters. The disease is caused by an inherited "looseness" in the hip joint and is greatly aggravated in overweight dogs. It is seen in almost all large breeds, including German shepherds, Labrador retrievers, and Rottweilers. However, the disorder is rare in greyhounds.

Skin Conditions: Such problems manifest themselves in a wide variety of malfunctions across numerous breeds. For instance, boxers are prone to various "lumps and bumps," including dermoid cysts, gum tumors, skin tumors, and mast cell tumors, while West Highland white terriers, golden retrievers, bull terriers, and beagles can suffer from allergic dermatitis.

Allergies

Allergies are a malfunction of the canine's immune system that triggers an over-response to specific environmental factors (called allergens). They are as common among dogs as they are among people (and particularly troubling among purebreds, who may be genetically predisposed to react to specific allergens). Common triggers include everything from flea saliva and ordinary grass to a particular ingredient in a commercially produced dog food. Canine reactions to allergies can range from mild discomfort to life-threatening emergencies (including allergen-induced swelling and constriction of the airway).

In most cases, the symptoms will manifest themselves in the skin. Itchiness of the paws, ears, abdomen, face, and rectal area are most common. Other problems include hair loss, hives, and gastrointestinal distress. Allergic reactions triggered by insect bites can be very serious and may lead to a life-threatening condition called anaphylactic shock. If you suspect your dog is allergic to something in its environment, consult your veterinarian.

Poisons

Dogs are programmed to investigate new things, which means they can sometimes consume dangerous substances. If you see your dog consume such an item, immediately (if possible) flush its mouth with water to remove any remaining residue. Contact your veterinarian immediately for further instructions, or call the American Society for the Prevention of Cruelty to Animals (ASPCA) Animal Poison Control Center at (888) 426-4435 (4ANIHELP). If you are instructed to visit a clinic, try to bring the toxin's container with you; this may provide vital information about the substance your dog has ingested.

✚ ☠ **Antifreeze:** Dogs are attracted by the sweet taste of antifreeze. ***Symptoms:*** Convulsions, wobbling, vomiting, coma, and sudden death. ***Treatment:*** If you are absolutely certain the dog has consumed antifreeze, induce vomiting (see page 170) and seek immediate medical attention. Even with prompt medical intervention, antifreeze poisoning is often fatal.

✚ ☠ **Aspirin:** Aspirin can be toxic to dogs if improperly administered. ***Symptoms:*** Staggering, pale gums, blood-tinged vomit, bloody diarrhea, and collapse. ***Treatment:*** If recently consumed, induce vomiting (see page 170) and administer a solution of water and baking soda to neutralize the aspirin. It should consist of 1–2 teaspoons (5–10 ml) of baking soda mixed with approximately 2 tablespoons (30 ml) of water. Seek immediate veterinary attention.

✚ **Chlorine:** If you have a swimming pool on your property, remember to keep chlorine locked away at all times. ***Symptoms:*** Runny or irritated eyes, red mouth, vomiting, diarrhea, mouth and tongue ulcerations. **Treatment:** Rinse eyes and mouth with water, provide plenty of water to drink, and seek immediate veterinary attention.

✚ ☠ **Lead:** This toxin is often found in old paint chips. **Symptoms:** Poor appetite, weight loss, vomiting, escalating to convulsion, paralysis, blindness, coma. **Treatment:** Lead poisoning symptoms build slowly over time. If you suspect your dog has it, ask your veterinarian to run a blood or urine test.

✚ ☠ **Turpentine:** Dogs can be poisoned by turpentine if they get it on their fur and try to lick it off. Turpentine can also be absorbed directly into the skin. **Symptoms:** Inflamed and irritated skin, vomiting, diarrhea, unsteadiness, coma. **Treatment:** Wash the affected area thoroughly, then seek immediate veterinary care.

✚ ☠ **Vermin Poisons:** Canines can be harmed by ingesting rat poison, or even by ingesting rats that have ingested rat poison. **Symptoms:** Convulsions, stiffness, hemorrhage, collapse. A common toxin in these products is warfarin, which disrupts the dog's blood clotting ability. **Treatment:** The best approach depends on the active ingredient in the poison. If possible, obtain its original packaging and seek immediate veterinary care.

⚠ **CAUTION:** Holiday poinsettias, which for decades were thought to be toxic to dogs, in fact pose no threat. However, mistletoe, holly, and Easter lilies can make canines violently ill.

To Induce Vomiting

Administering $^1/_2$ to 1 teaspoon ($2^1/_2$–5 ml) of syrup of ipecac (available in most drugstores) will cause the canine to vomit. Alternatively, a mixture consisting of 2 teaspoons (10 ml) of water and 2 teaspoons (10 ml) of 3 percent hydrogen peroxide should achieve the same effect.

Trauma

Canines are prone to numerous catastrophic malfunctions triggered by anything from inclement weather to unauthorized, uncontrolled interfaces with automobiles. In such situations, prompt, decisive action by the owner is the key first step toward full recovery.

✚ ☠ **Bloat:** A poorly understood condition usually seen in large, deep-chested breeds (Dobermans, Great Danes), bloat is seemingly associated with the rapid consumption of large amounts of dry food. Symptoms include nonproductive vomiting, severe discomfort, and swollen abdomen. Seek veterinary help immediately. Bloat is an extremely dangerous disorder that usually requires emergency surgery. If left untreated, it is fatal.

✚ ☠ **Blocked Airway:** Airway blockage (choking) can be triggered by traumatic injury, a foreign object in the throat, or a severe swelling or constriction (as from a too-tight collar) of the neck. Constriction injuries can also trigger pulmonary edema (buildup of fluid in the lungs). If a choking episode lasts for more than a few minutes, seek veterinary help. (See "The Heimlich Maneuver," page 183.)

✚ **Broken Bone(s):** Keep the dog calm. Do not try to apply a splint. If the bone has broken through the skin (a compound fracture), cover the injury with a bandage or clean cloth. Muzzle the dog (see page 181) so that it cannot inadvertently injure you during treatment or movement. Consult a veterinarian immediately.

✚ **Dog Bites:** All bites from another dog should be investigated by a veterinarian, because they can be more serious than they appear. Severe infection (becoming apparent after 24 hours) can accompany even a mild bite. Preliminary cleaning of the wound can be done with warm water and hydrogen peroxide. Be gentle and make sure the dog does not bite *you*.

✚ **Eye Injury:** If a foreign liquid is in the eye, flush with water or saline solution. Then seek professional help. Do not attempt to remove foreign objects (splinters, etc.) on your own. Virtually every eye problem merits immediate veterinary assistance.

✚ ☠ **Frostbite:** Remove the dog from the cold environment, then rewarm the affected tissues (usually the feet and/or ears) in warm water (approximately 104°F [40°C]). Do not rub or massage the tissue. Seek veterinary attention immediately.

✚ ☠ **Heatstroke:** Remove the dog from the heat. Place it in a cool bath, drench with cool water, or cover with a cool, water-soaked towel. Seek veterinary attention immediately.

✚ ☠ **Severe Laceration with Uncontrolled Bleeding:** Place a clean towel over the wound and then apply direct pressure to lessen loss of blood. Never attempt to apply a tourniquet. Seek veterinary care immediately.

✚ ☠ Severe Trauma and/or HBC (Hit by Car): Muzzle the dog to prevent it from injuring you (see page 181). Apply a clean cloth and pressure to any bleeding chest wounds. If breathing is severely labored, check mouth to make sure it is clear of obstructions. Lift into car using blanket or board as a stretcher. Seek veterinary care immediately.

✚ ☠ Snakebite: Do not apply a tourniquet or try to suck the venom out of the wound. To slow the circulation of the venom, limit your dog's activity as much as possible. Seek veterinary attention immediately. Snakebites are very painful, so handle the dog carefully.

Bugs in the System

A variety of internal and external parasites can invade your dog's systems, causing everything from acute discomfort to full system shutdown. Fortunately, most of these difficulties can be ended or avoided through careful maintenance and prompt medical attention.

Internal Parasites

✚ Giardia: This parasite causes mild enteritis and chronic diarrhea, particularly in puppies. Humans can also contract giardia (and suffer the same symptoms), though it is unclear whether the canine and human varieties of this parasite are the same. The right medication (administered by a veterinarian) will eliminate the problem.

✚ ☠ Heartworms: These mosquito-borne parasites can grow into foot-long worms that lodge in the right ventricle of the heart, causing significant damage to it and the lungs. Heartworms are deadly if untreated. Your vet-

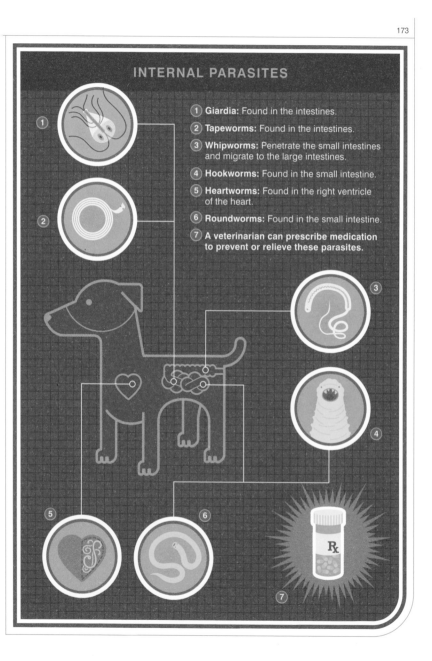

INTERNAL PARASITES

1. **Giardia:** Found in the intestines.
2. **Tapeworms:** Found in the intestines.
3. **Whipworms:** Penetrate the small intestines and migrate to the large intestines.
4. **Hookworms:** Found in the small intestine.
5. **Heartworms:** Found in the right ventricle of the heart.
6. **Roundworms:** Found in the small intestine.
7. **A veterinarian can prescribe medication to prevent or relieve these parasites.**

erinarian can prescribe a heartworm preventative, which may also prevent hookworms, roundworms, and whipworms.

✚ Hookworms: These small, blood-sucking parasites attach themselves to the walls of the small intestine. Signs include diarrhea, weakness, and anemia. They can be removed with a deworming medication. Prevention is easily accomplished by most heartworm medications.

✚ Roundworms: These intestinal parasites primarily afflict puppies less than 3 months old. Mature dogs may develop an immunity that prevents roundworm eggs from maturing into adults. However, the eggs will remain dormant in their bodies, waiting to infect the next generation. Puppy deworming medication destroys them, and standard heartworm medications stop initial infections. This parasite is potentially transmissible to humans.

✚ ☠ Tapeworms: The eggs of these parasites are most commonly transmitted via fleas, feces, and uncooked animal carcasses. There are several varieties, a few of which cause their canine hosts no lasting harm, but all should be promptly destroyed with deworming treatments. A few varieties produce eggs that may be transferred to humans and can lead to life-threatening cysts.

✚ Whipworms: These worms penetrate the small intestine as larvae, then migrate to the large intestine where they mature into adults. Signs include diarrhea, weight loss, and bloody stool. Whipworms can be eradicated with deworming compounds. Prevention is easily accomplished with many heartworm preventatives.

External Parasites

✚ Fleas: Though usually only an annoyance for most canines, these blood-sucking parasites can cause life-threatening blood loss in puppies and severely infested adults. Various shampoos, medicines, and topical applications can eliminate small-to-medium infestations (consult your veterinarian about the proper course of action). In some cases, fleas can cause an allergic reaction, transmit disease, and/or cause anemia.

⚠ CAUTION: Never use a topical flea treatment formulated for dogs on cats. Such products are highly toxic to felines.

✚ Flies/Fly-strike: Flies are a bigger problem than most people realize, particularly for dogs forced to live outside. Fly-strike is caused when numerous biting flies afflict the edges of the dog's ears, causing rawness, scabs, and, if no action is taken, infection. The area should be cleaned carefully with warm water and peroxide. Veterinary care may be necessary in advanced cases. Prevention is accomplished by daily application of a fly repellant. The surest cure for fly-strike is to bring the dog indoors.

✚ Lice: Lice can infest a dog by the thousands, causing severe itching. Eliminating them requires veterinary intervention.

✚ Mites: This parasite is responsible for an illness called mange. Demodectic or "red" mange produces small, hairless, irritated patches on the dog's coat. Sarcoptic mange or "scabies" triggers severe itching along with hair loss. Mites can also enter the ears, where they cause great discomfort and inevitably trigger bacterial infections. Mites should be treated by a veterinarian as soon as possible.

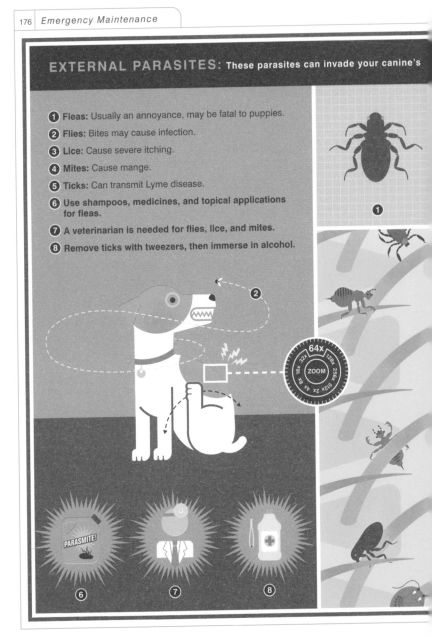

EXTERNAL PARASITES: These parasites can invade your canine's

1. **Fleas:** Usually an annoyance, may be fatal to puppies.
2. **Flies:** Bites may cause infection.
3. **Lice:** Cause severe itching.
4. **Mites:** Cause mange.
5. **Ticks:** Can transmit Lyme disease.
6. Use shampoos, medicines, and topical applications for fleas.
7. A veterinarian is needed for flies, lice, and mites.
8. Remove ticks with tweezers, then immerse in alcohol.

system, causing acute discomfort.

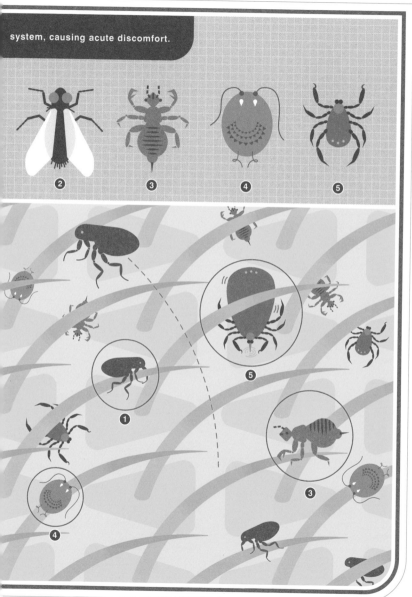

✚ Ticks: Remove them using tweezers. Try not to touch the ticks, as they can transmit disease to humans. Kill them by immersing them in alcohol. It is a good idea to inspect your dog for ticks after walking in the woods. Deer ticks can carry and transmit Lyme disease, which can lead to neurological and cardiac malfunction. (See "Contagious Diseases," page 162.)

Behavioral/Psychological Disorders

Not all malfunctions are hardware issues. Some dogs may develop software glitches that can only be resolved by specialists. Here are some of the most common.

Obsessive-Compulsive Behaviors: Obsessive behavior in dogs often mirrors the same disorder in humans. Affected canines will engage in repetitive behaviors (licking of the lower legs, tail chasing, pacing, fence running) that seem to serve no useful function and can even be harmful. In some cases, these may be triggered by separation anxiety, boredom, or other stress factors. Treatment by an animal behaviorist may help. Also, research suggests that the same antidepressants sometimes prescribed for humans with obsessive-compulsive disorder may alleviate dog symptoms as well. Consult your veterinarian before attempting such a course of treatment.

Phobias: Dogs, just like humans, can develop extreme, irrational fears of common objects and routine sensory stimuli—anything from the odor of a particular food to open flames to vacuum cleaners. The most common is a fear of thunderstorms or other loud noises. While many dogs are, to some degree, afraid of loud sounds, a few become so panic-stricken that they may burst through windows in an attempt to escape. In these extreme cases, an animal behaviorist (and a great deal of time) is needed to alleviate the problem.

Rage Syndrome: A fit that is similar to epilepsy, except that the dog involved displays uncontrollable aggression instead of seizing. This hereditary defect is seen in dogs of questionable or poorly managed genetic heritage and is in most cases untreatable. The only way to fully avoid this problem (which appears occasionally in such models as the springer spaniel and cocker spaniel) is to acquire your dog from a reputable breeder or other high-quality source.

Separation Anxiety: Dogs were designed for communal living, so spending long periods of time alone is, to some degree, always stressful for them. However, some canines take their discomfort to phobic levels, doing extensive damage to their owners' homes whenever they are left by themselves. Separation anxiety can also trigger other difficulties, such as obsessive-compulsive behaviors. Consult your veterinarian and/or an animal behaviorist about treatment options.

Emergency Transport Techniques

In the event that you need to transfer a canine that has been severely injured, use the following techniques to insure the safety of both the dog and the owner.

[1] Assess the scene. If the injured dog was hit by a car, be sure that the road is clear before attempting to help the animal.

[2] Approach the injured dog slowly. If it is growling, baring its teeth, or showing other signs of fear and/or aggression, be very careful. Remember, even a trusted family pet can lash out if suffering from severe pain.

[3] If the dog appears agitated, muzzle it using a commercial muzzle or a piece of fabric (panty hose work well) wound around the jaws and then tied behind the neck (Fig. A). A towel may be placed over the dog's head, in lieu of or in addition to a muzzle, to help calm the animal.

[4] If the dog is bleeding severely, place a bandage or clean cloth over the wound and apply pressure.

[5] Transport the dog to a vehicle using either a flat board, blanket, tarp, or other piece of sturdy cloth (Fig. B). Pull the dog carefully onto the transport vehicle (this is usually a two-person job). Smaller dogs may be moved in a box or crate.

181

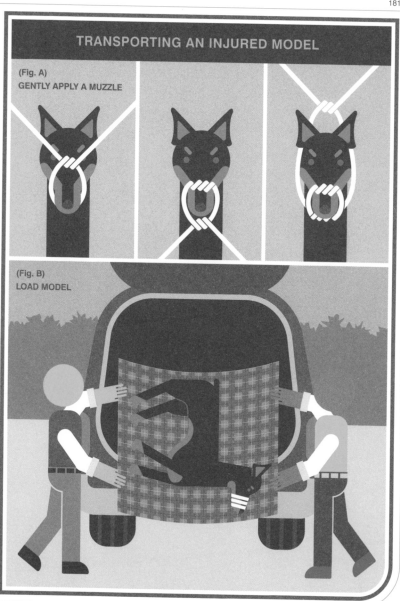

The Heimlich Maneuver

If a dog starts choking or appears to have difficulty breathing, it may have an obstruction in its throat. Employ the following maneuver to repair the problem.

[1] Open the dog's mouth and look at the back of its throat (Fig. A). If you can see the object causing the choking, remove it (Fig. B). If the dog is unconscious, pulling its tongue forward will give a better view and perhaps dislodge the object.

⚠ *CAUTION: Even an unconscious dog may bite on instinct. Be careful.*

[2] If the dog is small enough, pick it up and hold it by the hips with its head hanging down (Fig. C). For larger dogs, hold the hind legs in the air so its head hangs down. These techniques may cause the object to simply drop out. If not, you must perform the Heimlich maneuver.

[3] With the dog either standing or lying down, place your arms around its waist with hands clasped around its stomach. Close your hands into one fist and place it just behind the last rib.

[4] Compress the stomach by pushing up five times rapidly (Fig. D).

[5] Sweep your finger through the dog's mouth to see if the object has dislodged (Fig. E).

[6] If it hasn't, strike the dog sharply between the shoulder blades with the flat side of one hand (Fig. F), then repeat abdominal compressions. Alternate these procedures until the object is dislodged.

[7] If the object is dislodged but the dog no longer appears to be breathing, continue to the next section on artificial respiration and CPR.

Artificial Respiration and CPR

As with humans, dogs whose respiration and/or heart has stopped can be assisted with artificial respiration and cardiopulmonary resuscitation (CPR). However, these are last-ditch procedures that should only be attempted if you are absolutely sure the dog has stopped breathing. Place your hand on the left side of the chest to feel for a heartbeat (if you find one, the dog is still breathing). Alternatively, hold a mirror in front of the dog's nose and watch for condensation (if you see it, the dog is still breathing). Still another method is to place a cotton ball before the dog's nose and watch for even the slightest movement in the filaments.

⚠ *CAUTION: A dog's pulse cannot be taken at the neck. For additional instructions about monitoring the dog's heart rate, see page 158.*

[1] Inspect the airway for obstructions. Lay the dog on its side, tilt its head slightly back, pull the tongue out of the way, and use your fingers to feel for and remove obstructions. Perform the Heimlich maneuver if necessary (see previous page). If clearing the obstruction does not reinstate normal respiration, proceed to the next step.

[2] Be sure the dog's neck is straight. For medium to large dogs, place your hand around the muzzle, hold it closed, and place your mouth around its nose. For smaller dogs (under 30 pounds), your mouth should cover the dog's nose and lips (Fig. A).

[3] Give four or five quick, forceful breaths.

[4] Check for response. If normal breathing resumes, stop. If not, or if breathing is shallow, resume CPR. Give 20 breaths per minute for small dogs, or 20 to 30 breaths per minute for medium and large dogs.

[5] Check for heartbeat by placing your hand on the left side of the dog's chest. If none is detected, begin compressions along with rescue breathing.

[6] For most dogs, compressions can be performed while the animal lies on its side (Fig. B). The back is better for barrel-chested canines such as bulldogs. Whatever the approach, be sure the dog is on firm ground. Compressions will not be effective on a soft surface.

[7] For small dogs, place your palm and fingertips over the ribs at the point where the elbow meets the chest. Kneel down next to the dog, then compress the chest approximately 1 inch, twice per second. Alternate every five compressions with one breath. After 1 minute, check for heartbeat. If none is found, continue.

[8] For medium to large dogs, kneel down next to the canine, extend your elbows, and cup your hands on top of each other. Place hands over the ribs at the point where the dog's elbows meet the chest, then compress it 2 to 3 inches, one-and-a-half to two times per second. Alternate every five compressions with one breath. After 1 minute, check for heartbeat. If you find none, continue.

[9] For very large dogs (over 100 pounds or 45 kg), compress the chest 2 to 3 inches once per second, alternating every 10 compressions with breath. After 1 minute, check for heartbeat. If you find none, continue.

⚠ **CAUTION:** *The chances of reviving a canine with CPR are minimal. After 20 minutes of CPR, it is unlikely that the animal will be revived, even with professional intervention.*

Pet Insurance

Repairing a severely ill canine can be quite costly. In some cases, owners will choose to euthanize the dog rather than shoulder the expense. Pet insurance can help reduce the impact of unexpected maintenance costs. Just as with human health policies, owners pay a regular premium in exchange for help that ranges from coverage of annual checkups and immunizations to medical emergencies. Some companies offer annual preset spending limits, while others use deductibles. Premium payments, which are based on services offered and the condition/age of the canine, can range from $100 a year to more than $500.

Be advised that pet insurance is still a relatively rare phenomenon in the United States, with less than 500,000 American pet owners holding policies. Consult your veterinarian for information about reputable companies offering this service.

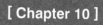

Chapter 10

Advanced Functions

If you have followed the information in the previous chapters, you now possess a healthy, well-behaved, semi-autonomous dog with all the programming necessary for a lifetime of companionship. However, home enthusiasts interested in even more add-ons can consult the following survey of options.

Home and Personal Defense

Training a dog to defend your home can be problematic. Though professional guard dog programs are available (ask your veterinarian and/or local breed club for references), in many cases this level of indoctrination is not necessary. Models created for defense (Rottweilers, German shepherds, Doberman pinschers, etc.) are in most cases hardwired to be suspicious of strangers, warn off trespassers, guard their home territory, and attack determined aggressors. Given the proper stimuli, these "killer aps" will self-activate. For many owners, in fact, the biggest challenge will be *controlling* such instincts, not developing them.

Owners of guard models would be better served by investing in extensive obedience training. This will provide the sorts of downloads needed in the real world: the ability to control the canine in public situations; to have it come promptly when called; and, perhaps most importantly, to make it instantly stop whatever it might be doing.

⚠ **EXPERT TIP:** *The dog's most useful intruder repellant is its bark. In many cases, small and nervous dogs make the best home defense systems because they will raise the alarm at the slightest external stimulus.*

Insurance Issues

Be advised that some insurance companies refuse to write homeowners policies for clients who own certain dog models deemed to be "dangerous." The list varies from company to company, but usually includes all the common guarding varieties such as pit bulls, Rottweilers, mastiffs, Doberman pinschers, and German shepherds. Owning a mixed breed that contains these particular bloodlines may also cause an insurance company to refuse coverage. A potential client's particular dog need not have been involved in any incidents; the mere fact that it belongs to a particular breed can make obtaining insurance difficult. At present, there is no legislation in the United States outlawing or regulating this practice.

Contests

If you would like to test the performance of your model against those of other enthusiasts, there are plenty of events in which you and your canine can participate.

Agility Competitions (Fig. A): In this test of training, intelligence, and canine stamina, owner-guided dogs race the clock as they tackle complex obstacle courses filled with hurdles, tunnels, and jumps. Models ranging from purebreds to mutts can participate, and there are separate divisions for different dog sizes. However, the canines must be young and fit, because agility events can be very demanding.

Dog Shows (Fig. B): Hundreds of dog shows, big and small, are held in the United States throughout the year. The best-known are conducted under the auspices of the American Kennel Club and open only to AKC-registered pure-

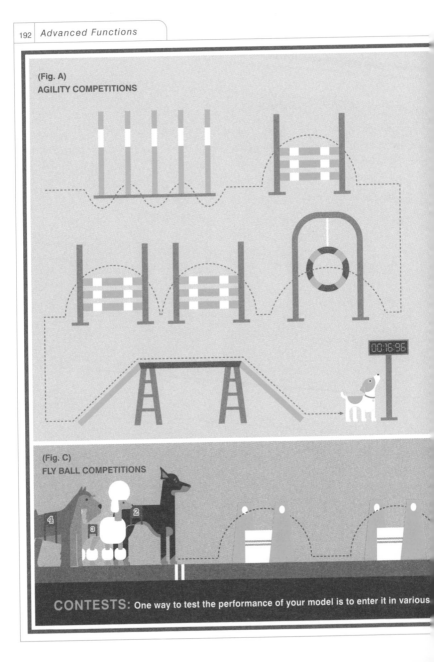

(Fig. A)
AGILITY COMPETITIONS

00:16:96

(Fig. C)
FLY BALL COMPETITIONS

CONTESTS: One way to test the performance of your model is to enter it in various

(Fig. B)
DOG SHOWS

ompetitions. Judges evaluate agility, obedience, beauty, and other desirable traits.

breds. Dogs are judged on their conformation to their "breed standard" (a multipage set of technical specs outlining a model's appropriate physical makeup). Enthusiasts can attend or participate in specialty shows (encompassing only a single breed), all-breed shows (large events at which almost any AKC-recognized model can participate), and matches (essentially practice gatherings popular with novice owners and young dogs). Dog show competitors are judged on how well they adhere to their breed standard and little else.

Fly Ball Competitions (Fig. C): This most exciting of all canine sports is essentially a relay race in which teams of four dogs compete against each other and the clock. Each dog runs a course of hurdles to reach a "fly ball box." The dog presses a lever at the bottom of the box, which shoots a tennis ball into the air. The dog grabs the ball and dashes back to the start/ finish line, sending the next dog on his team down the course. Dogs compete in different size divisions, though, of course, canines built for speed (Border collies, Jack Russell terriers) have a distinct advantage.

Obedience Competitions: These events test both the intelligence of the dogs and the training ability of their owners. Contests include distance control (getting canines to unfailingly obey commands, even when the person giving them is far away), scent discrimination (selecting one differently scented object from among many), heel work, and other even more complicated maneuvers.

Breed-specific Gatherings: Organizations dedicated to individual breeds often hold their own local, regional, and national rallies, many with events geared to the strengths of their particular model. For instance, retrieving competitions for Labrador and other retrievers; simulated underground prey pursuits for West Highland terriers; and races for Jack Russell terriers.

Hardware Modifications

Purebred owners sometimes amputate (dock) the tails and trim (crop) portions of the ears of various breeds so that they conform to a particular aesthetic standard. For instance, the ears of Doberman pinschers, American Staffordshire terriers, and boxers are, in their natural state, disarmingly floppy. Surgery must be performed to give them their intimidating points. Likewise, boxers, Doberman Pinschers, and other breeds often have most of their tails docked. This is usually accomplished between 3 and 5 days of age.

Neither of these procedures is necessary for the health and happiness of the animal. Indeed, in recent years a backlash against such "cosmetic surgery" has developed, with some even charging that it amounts to animal cruelty. As of now the decision remains a personal one—though, of course, any such procedure should be done only under a veterinarian's care.

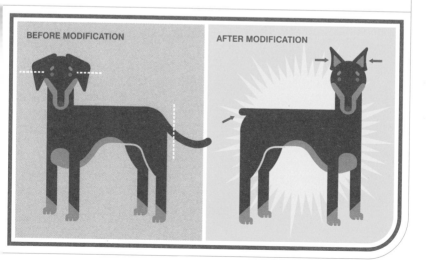

BEFORE MODIFICATION AFTER MODIFICATION

There is one form of elective surgery that can actually *improve* the health and safety of your dog. Canines have an extra, rudimentary nail, called a dewclaw, located on each foot. It performs no function and on the hind limbs often isn't even connected to supporting bone. Dewclaws can pose a problem for dogs who spend any amount of time outdoors. They can snag on underbrush, causing painful, bloody injuries. They can be surgically removed from puppies at 3 to 5 days of age, and from older dogs during spaying/neutering or anytime thereafter. The procedure is minor and recovery rapid.

Reproduction

For a number of reasons, chief among them pet overpopulation, the breeding of dogs is not recommended by most veterinarians and trainers. However, if you own a purebred (some of whom are sold on condition that they be bred at least once), here is a brief overview of what to expect during the mating and reproduction process.

Selecting a Mate

Puppies are strongly influenced by the mental and physical strengths—and shortcomings—of their parents. For this reason, it is important to pick a strong breeding partner for your dog. Here are some of the most important factors to consider.

■ Choose a mate from a reputable, experienced breeder.

■ Make sure the mate is AKC-registered, or registered with another reputable breed association.

■ Carefully investigate the genetic heritage of the potential mate. Be extremely wary if information about the canine's lineage isn't available.

■ Check the potential mate carefully for genetic abnormalities. If there are any questions, a veterinary checkup may be in order.

■ Be wary of any personality foibles, which may be reflected in the puppies. Be particularly skeptical of potential mates that show undue aggression.

Mating

A dog should be at least 20 months old before it begins to mate. Most female dogs go into heat (estrus) twice each year. During the middle portion of estrus, the female will become receptive to male dogs. She will indicate her preparedness by standing still among male dogs and "flagging" her tail (moving it to one side).

When this occurs, the female dog should be introduced to a male dog (the mating will be more successful if it takes place on the male's territory). If the dogs appear compatible and the female is receptive, mating can be allowed to proceed. Though ejaculation usually takes

less than a minute after coupling, the dogs may remain connected or "tied" for as long as 40 minutes. Shortly after ejaculation, the male will dismount and, still connected to the female, may turn so that he is facing away from her. This uncomfortable-looking maneuver is natural and to be expected. The mating can be repeated every second day, until the female rejects the male.

EXPERT TIP: *Female dogs can be impregnated by more than one dog. In theory, a single litter could contain puppies with several different fathers.*

Pregnancy

On average, canine pregnancies last 63 days, though the duration can vary from 59 to 66 days. At 5 weeks, the mother's nipples will become enlarged and her abdomen will swell. At 7 weeks, her mammary glands will enlarge. In the days before the birth, these glands may also secrete watery milk. During pregnancy the mother's body weight may increase as much as 50 percent (a little over 30 percent is more typical).

Prenatal Monitoring

Your veterinarian can detect a pregnancy at 3 to 4 weeks via ultrasound, X-ray, or abdominal palpitation. Though a well-balanced diet for the mother is important, the volume of food need not be increased during the first 6 weeks. After that time, however, food intake should increase until, by week 8 or 9, the mother eats as much as double her usual amount (provided in small, multiple meals). Special vitamin supplements may also be prescribed. Mild exercise can be maintained to help keep the dog physically fit.

Preparing for Birth

Though in most cases birthing can be accomplished at home, it is wise to discuss the situation with your vet in advance. Also, certain breeds, such as bulldogs, have such difficult vaginal births that cesarean section deliveries are recommended.

Approximately 10 days before the birth, provide the mother with a "whelping box" where she can deliver her litter. It should have walls high enough to corral the puppies, but low enough so the mother can leave easily. It should also be large enough for the mother to lie down in during nursing. Cover the bottom with soft towels and place the box in a quiet area.

Birth

During the first stage of labor, the female may pant, whimper, lick herself energetically, and repeatedly get up and lie down in her whelping box. As the situation progresses, she may lie down on her side with her head up, looking at her hindquarters. Visible straining will be evident. Puppies will usually appear head first (though tail first is not uncommon), enclosed in a bluish membrane. Once birth is accomplished, the mother will tear open the membrane, chew through the umbilical cord, and vigorously lick the puppy to stimulate respiration. Shortly after the birth of each puppy, its individual placenta will also pass. Births can occur from 30 minutes to 2 hours apart.

⚠ *CAUTION: Inexperienced mothers may not chew open the membrane or cut the umbilical cord, so be prepared to help her. In general, the larger the dog breed, the bigger the litter. Toy breeds often have one to four puppies, while larger breeds can have eight, twelve, or more.*

Canine Travel

It is not uncommon for users to transport their dogs via automobile or plane to various destinations. When traveling with your dog, use the following handling guidelines to minimize damage to your model.

Automobile Travel

It is acceptable for larger dogs to ride in a seat, like a human passenger (Fig. A). If your dog has never done this before, consider making one or two short "practice" excursions to be sure the canine keeps its place and does not try to roam around the car. Smaller dogs may prefer to be transported in their sleeping crates, as this provides a secure refuge from a strange situation (Fig. B). Be aware that all dogs are fascinated by the smells they encounter when they stick their noses out the window of a moving car. It is acceptable to indulge this desire, but never leave the window open so far that the dog can jump or fall out (Fig. C).

During long car trips, allow the dog to make regular rest and exercise stops (always leash it before opening the car door). Bring along food, water, and treats in a separate container. If your dog is prone to getting carsick, your veterinarian may recommend medication (bringing the dog on a few short "practice" trips may prevent the problem altogether).

⚠ *CAUTION: Never, for any reason, leave your dog alone in a car. Changes in outdoor temperatures are unpredictable and can lead to stress, hypothermia, heat exhaustion, and worse.*

AUTOMOBILE TRANSPORT

(Fig. A)
LARGER MODELS CAN SIT UP FRONT

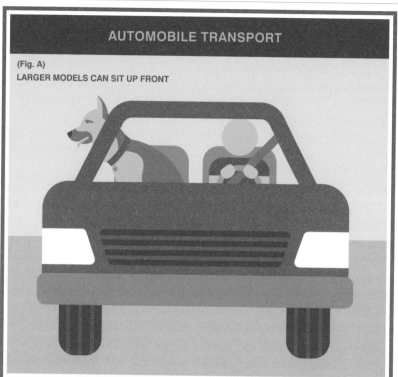

(Fig. B)
USE CARRIER FOR SMALLER MODELS

(Fig. C)
KEEP WINDOW OPEN PARTIALLY

Air Travel

If possible, avoid traveling with your dog by airplane. The only exception to this rule is if the dog is very small and permitted to fly in the cabin, secured inside a travel carrier that can fit under your seat (an industry-wide airline regulation). Larger dogs must travel in the aircraft's hold—a rough, frightening, and potentially dangerous practice. The environment is extremely uncomfortable, and the dog could die of overheating in the event of a long flight delay. There is also the ever-present danger of its carrier being misrouted to the wrong destination.

If you have no choice but to travel by air, familiarize yourself with the airline's pet transportation protocols well in advance of the flight. Procure an airline-approved shipping kennel and make sure all necessary paperwork is completed. Try to select a nonstop flight and, if possible, do not fly during the hottest (or coldest) part of the day. Travel on the same flight as your dog, if possible, and inform at least one flight attendant and the pilot that your canine is in the hold.

⚠️ **CAUTION:** *Veterinarians can prescribe tranquilizers during travel, but this will place your dog under the influence of an unfamiliar drug while stowed in the hold, far from help should something go wrong. Discuss the risks and benefits with your veterinarian before proceeding.*

Old Age

The age at which a dog can be considered elderly varies widely among models. In general, the larger the dog, the more quickly it declines. For instance, a Great Dane could be considered "senior" at age 5, while a smaller toy poodle would still be spry at twice that age. Remember, however, that just because a dog is chronologically old doesn't mean that an endless series of malfunctions is in store. In many cases an elderly dog can enjoy many healthy, active, pain-free years.

One of the best ways to prolong the life and improve the functions of an elderly dog is to carefully regulate its fuel intake. Older dogs exercise less and thus need fewer calories. And since age reduces their ability to digest and absorb nutrients, high-quality food specifically formulated for their needs is a necessity. Excessive amounts of protein, phosphorus, and sodium can aggravate kidney and heart problems, so most such foods contain smaller amounts of higher-quality protein, along with reduced quantities of other elements. Levels of vitamins, zinc, fatty acids, and fiber, however, are increased.

Common Age-Related Malfunctions

- Gradual decline of auditory sensors
- Degradation of visual sensors caused primarily by lens deterioration or cataracts
- Gastrointestinal distress caused by lack of tolerance for dietary changes
- Loss of muscle and bone mass, cartilage deterioration, and arthritis
- Hair whitening and loss
- Heart murmurs triggered by scarred or poorly functioning heart valves
- Incontinence triggered by loss of kidney function and bladder control; decreasing mental function may also cause the dog to "forget" its house-training

Obsolescence and Deactivation

When compared to other consumer items, the service lifetime of a dog is quite impressive. Larger models can function for a decade, while compact units may approach twice that. But even though your dog will almost certainly outlast your car, television, and computer, its time with you may still seem startlingly, even heartbreakingly, brief.

This is because while many people profess to "love" their car, television, or computer, with dogs they truly mean it. While canines can be programmed to do many useful things, their most important application is as a companion and friend. When the time approaches to part with that friend, owners may feel great trepidation. Yet this is also the time when they can render their greatest service to a loyal canine companion.

No two situations are alike, but in most cases an elderly dog should be maintained for as long as it remains in relatively good health and free of severe, chronic pain. Though the animal may be a shadow of its former self, rest assured that this is more troubling to its human companions than to the animal. Nothing in the dog's vast programming base corresponds to the human emotions of regret and painful nostalgia. In other words, an elderly dog does not fret over days gone by and days to come. It lives solely for the here and now.

That fact is very important when considering how to handle a canine's final days. In some cases an elderly dog will deactivate at a time and place of its own choosing. But in situations where declining health incapacitates the dog or causes it to suffer, the owner must act on its behalf. When the pain and disability in a dog's life seems to outweigh the pleasure, and when there is no reasonable hope of recovery, euthanasia should be considered. This procedure is painless and can be performed at the veterinarian's office. At the appropriate time the dog receives an overdose of anesthetic that causes almost immediate unconsciousness, followed rapidly by death.

Coping with the deactivation of a canine companion can be difficult. In some cases, the mourning period may be as long as that for the loss of a human. There is nothing unnatural about such feelings. National and local grief counseling groups are available to help bereaved dog owners through this period.

Rest assured that, given enough time, the pain of loss will pass. It will be replaced by many happy memories, the warranty for which can never expire.

[Appendix]

Troubleshooting

For easy access, this section contains answers to frequently asked questions about common canine behavior issues, malfunctions, and quirks. When problems arise with your model, this should be the first place you look.

SYMPTOM:	EXPLANATION:
Dog has consumed an unauthorized, indigestible item.	If the item is fairly small (say, the size of a marble), non-toxic, and smooth, watch the dog's stool for the next few days to see if it passes. If it doesn't, contact your veterinarian. An X-ray may be necessary to find the object and decide on a course of action. However, if the object poses a threat of internal injury (jagged edges, potentially toxic, uncomfortably large), contact your veterinarian immediately. Emergency surgery may be required to remove it. ⚠ **CAUTION:** *If your dog consumes string, tinsel, or a similar substance, and you notice it protruding from the rectum, do not attempt to pull it out. This risks internal damage. Contact your veterinarian immediately.*
Dog hates men in hats, little girls in dresses, women with high-pitched voices, or some other odd subset of the human race.	Some dogs are genetically predisposed to fearful behavior. However, others can acquire such fear if they undergo a traumatic experience during their early puppyhood. For instance, if a puppy has a frightening encounter with a man in a hat, that experience may ingrain itself so deeply that it forevermore fears and hates men in hats. This reaction can also be more general; an afflicted dog may simply despise all men. The usual treatment method is desensitization: gradual exposure to the thing the dog fears. This can be a rather lengthy, involved process, so consult a trainer, veterinarian, or animal behaviorist before attempting it.

SYMPTOM:	EXPLANATION:
Dog destroys furnishings or other household items when left alone.	This common (albeit expensive) problem can be caused by several things. The dog may be suffering from severe separation anxiety and taking out its angst on the home furnishings. It may suffer from barrier frustration, attacking doors and/or windows in an attempt to get outside. Or the dog may simply be bored. In such cases, the destructive activity has no particular focus. The canine may assault a chair on Monday and a piano leg on Tuesday. Mild cases of separation anxiety can sometimes be treated by giving the dog more exercise (a tired canine is infinitely less destructive) or providing it with interesting toys. However, in some cases this fear approaches phobic proportions. Medication and/or intervention by an animal behaviorist may be required.
Dog is terrified of thunder-storms.	The first step to alleviating this very common problem is to speak to the dog in an upbeat and sympathetic voice. Your reassuring tone will suggest that there is nothing to be afraid of. Distract the dog from the storm by playing with it or offering it a treat. In some cases this works, but in others (extreme cases in which the dog may break furniture or vomit from fear) the services of an animal behaviorist may be required.
Dog barks whenever someone talks on the phone.	This common behavior is usually triggered by a simple misunderstanding. The dog does not realize the person on the phone is talking to someone else. Since there is no one else in the room, the dog thinks the person must be talking to it—and it is responding.

SYMPTOM:	EXPLANATION:
Dog loathes the mail carrier and greets him with violent barking.	Highly territorial dogs seem to despise these civil servants with a special vigor. The reason is because they arrive at more or less the same time every day, come right up to the front door, and sometimes actually slide objects through it. This puts a dog's territorial defense programming into overdrive. Even worse, the mail carrier inevitably departs soon after the dog begins barking, leading it to conclude that it "repelled" the invader. Thus, what looks to humans like pointless aggression can be effective strategy to a canine.
Crate-trained puppy barks incessantly while confined.	First, make sure the puppy is receiving a proper amount of exercise before being crated, that its sleeping arrangements are comfortable, and that it has at least one chew toy. Then, do something that many owners find very hard—ignore the barking. It is natural for puppies who find themselves alone to call out, and it takes time for a dog to learn that this is unacceptable behavior. If you go to the crated puppy when it barks, it learns that such behavior brings attention. And if you hold out for a while, then go to the dog, you teach that prolonged, relentless barking brings results. Never go to the crated dog while it barks. Wait until it stops, then go.
Dog is extremely shy around strangers and/or other dogs.	Some dogs are simply shy by nature. Others were made that way by a bad experience during puppyhood. To improve the situation, one can stage low-key encounters with strangers (strangers to the dog, not to the owner). The visitor should be very friendly and nonthreatening. Treats should be offered. The dog should be praised for showing even the slightest bit of self-confidence. Repeating this exercise may reinforce the idea that meeting new people and animals is not something to be feared—or feared as much.

SYMPTOM:	EXPLANATION:
Dog displays a great deal of aggression toward other canines.	Some breeds are genetically predisposed to canine aggression. Most of the guarding breeds do not play well with others, and terriers are legendary for their lack of social skills. If your dog is thrust into situations where it encounters other canines, it is your responsibility to keep the unit under control through careful obedience training and leashing. If the dog only becomes aggressive with canines walking near its home or, perhaps, encroaching on its yard, then the source of its belligerence may be a strongly developed sense of territoriality. Such a dog may be able to consort with other dogs on neutral territory (the sidewalk, a dog park) with no difficulty at all.
Dog digs up the yard.	A common problem among bored outdoor dogs, excessive digging can be stopped simply by making the canine an *indoor* pet. Another approach is to designate a particular part of the yard as okay for digging and try to confine the activity there. Seed the area with toys and treats, then actively praise the canine when it begins turning that section of earth. To prevent digging altogether, pick up feces from around the yard, deposit them in canine-excavated holes, and cover them with a small amount of dirt. They will make an unpleasant (and, perhaps, behavior-changing) surprise for the dog when it attempts to resume its excavation work. Supervision will always be necessary to make sure a digging dog does not return to free-range excavation. This behavior can be particularly strong among terriers and terrier mixes, who were created to dig small animals out of their underground lairs (the name terrier means, literally, "earth dog.")

SYMPTOM:	EXPLANATION:
After meals, dog wipes its muzzle on the carpet.	This programmed behavior is another remnant of the wolf operating system. After dining on a kill, wolves routinely rub their faces on the ground to remove blood and offal from their faces. Domestic canines, even though their meal-times are usually much less messy, do the same thing.
Dog jumps on owner, family members, and/or visitors.	In most cases, this is simply an overexuberant greet-ing. Correct the problem not by shouting at the dog or "kneeing" (using a knee to deliver a blow to the dog's chest), but by ignoring the behavior. Make no reaction at all, for good or ill. Just move away from the dog so that it cannot continue. In most cases, the dog will eventually stop. Another alternative is to command the dog to sit when it seems about to jump.
Dog greets visitors with a bizarre, snarl-like expression.	Most canines are capable of a "smile"—a combination greeting/submission gesture. In some cases, dogs who are particularly excited about greeting someone will overdo it, producing a ghastly, all-teeth-bared expres-sion that can be intimidating to anyone who does not understand what the dog is feeling. ⚠ **CAUTION:** *If you encounter a strange dog wearing this expression, assume it is hostile until it proves otherwise.*
Dog humps people and inanimate objects.	In many cases mounting is done to display dominance, not necessarily for sexual reasons. Should your dog initiate such behavior, push him down immediately. The mounting of inanimate objects may be performed by young canines—both male and female models—to relieve sexual frustration.

SYMPTOM:	EXPLANATION:
Dog attempts to chase cars, joggers, bikers, and any other fast-moving object.	The sight of any speeding object will activate remnants of the wolf operating system associated with the pursuit of prey. The best way to stop this behavior is to keep the dog indoors, in a securely fenced yard, or on a leash. All dogs possess this pursuit protocol, but in some models the urge can be almost overwhelming. Greyhounds and cairn terriers, among others, are so keen to chase that they cannot be trusted off their leads in public for any reason. **EXPERT TIP:** *If you ever find yourself pursued by a dog, the best tactic is to stop, turn, and then face it. Most such dogs have been overwhelmed by their chase programming. Removing the stimuli can cause the units to automatically reset.*
Dog eats grass.	This behavior is as normal as the human consumption of lettuce. Canines seem to need the roughage, though they derive little nutrient value from it. In rare circumstances, nauseated dogs will consume large amounts of grass to induce vomiting.
Dog eats its own feces.	This behavior, known as pica, is most commonly seen in puppies and dogs on diets, both of whom may seek more nutrient or caloric value from undigested particles in the stool. Commercial products can be placed on the dog's food that will impart a bitter taste to its feces. Alternatively, lace feces left in the yard with jalapeño sauce. This is best done under cover of darkness, to prevent queries from neighbors.

SYMPTOM:	EXPLANATION:
Dog drags its hindquarters across the ground.	This is usually due to irritation of the rectal area, often caused by anal gland problems. (See "Exterior Maintenance," page 129.) Other triggers include allergic skin diseases and, in some cases, tapeworms.
Dog drools excessively.	Though it is rarely mentioned in breed guides, many canine models drool. Indeed, Saint Bernards and mastiffs are famous—or, rather, infamous—for their expectoratory excess. The phenomenon can be particularly pronounced after exercise. Nothing can be done to stop it, although some owners carry paper towels to keep their models presentable during long walks.
	⚠ **CAUTION:** *If a dog who normally does not drool suddenly starts, watch the behavior carefully and contact your veterinarian if it does not end quickly. It could indicate dental problems, sickness, or ingestion of a toxin.*
Dog greets visitors and even members of its immediate family by urinating.	Releasing a small (or not-so-small) amount of urine is a common submission gesture among canines. Also, dogs with relatively weak bladders who become overstimulated (often when guests visit) may lose urinary tract integrity. Barring a medical problem, the best approach is to keep comings and goings as low-key as possible. For instance, when arriving home from work, avoid making a huge fuss, vigorously petting the dog, and speaking to it in an excited voice. Give a perfunctory initial greeting and allow the dog time to adjust to the new situation before providing a warmer response. Instruct all visitors to do the same.

SYMPTOM:	EXPLANATION:
Dog lifts its leg to urinate.	This common behavior can perplex the novice dog owner. Male canines, as they reach sexual maturity, often begin to use sprays of urine to mark the boundaries of what they perceive as their territory. (See "House-Training," page 84.) In order to make themselves appear large and intimidating, they hike their legs to place the stream as high as possible. The higher the mark—or so its creator wants others to think—the bigger the dog. Females will occasionally engage in this behavior. Some males neutered before sexual maturity never do.
Adult, house-trained dog begins urinating in the home.	Healthy canines, particularly males, mark the boundaries of their territory with urine. Unfortunately, they sometimes do this indoors. Once a dog "marks" an indoor spot, it may return to it again and again, guided and stimulated by the smell of previous visits. It is important to clean such areas with an odor-cutting compound (available at pet stores). If your dog has not been neutered, have a veterinarian perform this procedure immediately. Then observe the dog carefully as it makes its rounds through the house. If you catch the dog trying to urinate in its favorite spot, immediately escort it outside. Repeat until it understands the new protocol. ⚠️ **CAUTION:** *Accidental indoor urination can also be a symptom of physical ailments. See page 165.*

SYMPTOM:	EXPLANATION:
Dog's coat seems dull.	If the dog has no apparent medical problems, an improper diet may be to blame. Some foods, particularly homemade ones, may lack a proper balance of vitamins, minerals, and/or essential fats. Changing to a higher quality, more readily digestible food may be the solution.
Dog makes an alarming series of gagging/snorting sounds that last for 30 to 60 seconds.	This phenomenon is called reverse sneezing—a series of rapid, spasmodic inhalations caused by irritation of the pharynx. Severe cases can be treated with drugs, but in most instances it is no more dangerous than a sneezing fit.
Dog shows no interest in you or your family, refuses to perform any useful tasks, and displays subpar intelligence.	Consult your veterinarian. You may have accidentally acquired a cat.

Technical Support

The following organizations offer valuable information and/or services to dog owners.

Animal Poison Control Center **(888) 426-4435**

Run by the American Society for the Prevention of Cruelty to Animals (ASPCA), the Animal Poison Control Center is staffed 24 hours a day, 7 days a week by veterinarians. They can advise during poison emergencies, provide treatment protocols, and even consult with clients' personal veterinarians. There may be a $45 charge for the service, depending on the circumstances, so have your credit card ready.

1-800-Save-A-Pet.com
(800) 728-3273
A national, nonprofit clearinghouse for mixed and purebred dogs in need of homes. Web-based search service allows for the easy location of rescue groups in particular areas.

American Animal Hospital Association
Member Service Center
(800) 883-6301
Can provide information on AAHA-approved veterinary hospitals in your area. For more information, visit www.healthypet.com.

AMERICAN KENNEL CLUB: AKC Breeder Referral Service
(900) 407-7877
For a free Dog Buyer's Educational Packet, call AKC Customer Service at (919) 233-9767. For information on breed rescue organizations throughout the United States, visit ww.akc.org/breeds/rescue.cfm.

AKC Canine Legislation Department
(919) 816-3720
E-mail contact: doglaw@akc.org
Monitors federal, state, and local legislation relating to dog ownership.

AKC Companion Animal Recovery
(800) 252-7894
E-mail contact: found@akc.org
A 24-hour hotline to which owners of dogs with microchip identification can report their lost canines and/or receive information about their whereabouts.

American Society for the Prevention of Cruelty to Animals
(212) 876-7700
www.aspca.org
Founded in 1866, the ASPCA is the oldest humane organization in the Western Hemisphere. Among many other things, it provides humane education, advice on obtaining medical services, and support for animal shelters.

American Veterinary Medical Association
(847) 925-8070
www.avma.org
A not-for-profit association of roughly 70,000 veterinarians that can provide information on AVMA-accredited facilities in your area.

Humane Society of the United States
(202) 452-1100
www.hsus.org
Animal advocacy and information clearinghouse covering such topics as pet adoption, care, and rights.

National Pesticide Information Center
(800) 858-7378
Offers free information about the toxicity of common compounds such as lawn care and gardening products.

Petswelcome.com
Extensive Internet site offering comprehensive information on traveling with dogs, including listings of hotels that take pets; kennels; amusement park pet facilities; and how to cope with emergencies on the road.

Glossary of Terms

■ **Allergen:** A substance that can induce an allergic reaction.

■ **Allergy:** A hypersensitivity in the immune response system. Symptoms may vary from minor skin irritation and gastrointestinal disturbances to a violent, sometimes life-threatening reaction called anaphylactic shock.

■ **Anal sacs:** Glands bracketing the anus that secrete a pungent fluid during bowel movements. Used by dogs to identify each other.

■ **Anestrus:** The sexually inactive period for female dogs between estrus cycles.

■ **Breed:** Group of dogs who exhibit a particular set of physical/mental characteristics developed through selective mating.

■ **Conformation:** The primary judging criteria at dog shows. Winning dogs "conform" most closely to the physical standard of their breeds.

■ **Cropping:** Trimming the ears to conform to an artificial aesthetic standard.

■ **Dewclaws:** A vestigial nail located on the inside of each canine leg. Often surgically removed.

■ **Docking:** The surgical removal of most of the tail.

■ **Dysplasia:** Abnormal bone or tissue development. Most commonly seen as hip dysplasia, a hereditary condition in which the hip joint fails to develop properly.

■ **Estrus:** Period in which a female dog is in heat.

■ **Hackles:** Neck and back hair.

■ **Heat:** Period in which a female dog is receptive to mating. See *Estrus*.

■ **Lipoma:** A benign fat tumor extremely common in older canines.

■ **Mutts:** Dogs of no specific "pure" breed; also known as mongrels or mixed breeds.

■ **Muzzle:** The projecting portion of the canine face, including the mouth, nose, and jaws. Also a fastening or covering for this part of the dog, used to prevent biting and/or eating.

■ **Neutering:** Sterilization of a male dog via removal of the testicles.

■ **Parasites:** Internal and external life forms that use other animals (in this case, dogs) as hosts. Includes, but is not confined to, heartworms, fleas, tapeworms, and mites.

■ **Proestrus:** The period just before a female dog enters estrus (heat).

■ **Purebreds:** Dogs belonging to a specific breed produced through selective mating.

■ **Sight Hounds:** Hunting dogs such as borzois and greyhounds that track prey primarily by sight.

■ **Spaying:** Sterilization of a female dog via hysterectomy.

■ **Stripping:** The removal of dead hairs from a dog's coat.

■ **Tricolor:** A canine coat with three colors.

■ **Whelping:** The act of giving birth.

■ **Withers:** The point just behind the neck from which a dog's height is determined.

Index

OWNER'S CERTIFICATE

Congratulations! Now that you've studied all the instructions in this manual, you are fully prepared to maintain your new dog. With the proper care and attention, your model will provide you with many years of fun and happiness. Enjoy!

Owner's name

_____

Model's name

_____

Model's date of acquisition

_____

Model's breed, if any

_____

Model's gender

_____

Model's coat color

_____

About the Authors:

A veterinarian for 25 years and operator of Indianapolis's Broad Ripple Animal Clinic for 22 years, **DR. DAVID BRUNNER** specializes in treating small animals—cats and dogs. He has two daughters, Molly and Kendell, and two black Labrador retrievers, Lucy and Noel, both of whom come to work with him every day.

SAM STALL is the coauthor of *As Seen On TV: 50 Amazing Products and the Commercials That Made Them Famous* and *Dirty Words of Wisdom*. He resides in Indianapolis with his three terrier mixed-breeds, Tippy, Katie, and Gracie, as well as his wife, Jami (who has no terrier blood whatsoever), and their cat, Ted.

About the Illustrators:

PAUL KEPPLE and **JUDE BUFFUM** are better known as the Philadelphia-based studio **HEADCASE DESIGN**. Their work has been featured in many design and illustration publications, such as *American Illustration, Communication Arts*, and *Print*. Paul worked at Running Press Book Publishers for several years before opening Headcase in 1998. Both graduated from the Tyler School of Art, where they now teach. While illustrating this book, Jude acquired a Boston terrier named Huxley, which he has since programmed to sit, stay, roll over, and mix cocktails. Paul's dog, an imaginary Jack Russell named Crackers, was last seen romancing a pair of running shoes.